Global Conscience

Global Conscience

Douglas Roche

NOVALIS

© 2007 Novalis, Saint Paul University, Ottawa, Canada

Cover design and layout: Audrey Wells
Cover image: Ina Peters/iStockphotos

Business Offices:
Novalis Publishing Inc.
10 Lower Spadina Avenue, Suite 400
Toronto, Ontario, Canada
M5V 2Z2

Novalis Publishing Inc.
4475 Frontenac Street
Montréal, Québec, Canada
H2H 2S2

Phone: 1-800-387-7164
Fax: 1-800-204-4140
E-mail: books@novalis.ca
www.novalis.ca

Library and Archives Canada Cataloguing in Publication

Roche, Douglas, 1929–
   Global conscience / Douglas Roche.

Includes index.
ISBN 978-2-89507-908-8

    1. World citizenship. 2. International cooperation. 3. Peace.
4. Security, International. 5. International relations. 6. International
agencies. I. Title.

JZ1320.5.R62 2006   327.1'72   C2007-903269-9

Printed in Canada.

We acknowledge the financial support of the Government of Canada through
the Book Publishing Industry Development Program (BPIDP) for our publishing
activities.

5   4   3   2   1   11   10   09   08   07

For Jonathan Granoff

Friend and Mentor

Contents

Acknowledgements... 9

Foreword, by Roméo Dallaire 11

Introduction: Lifting Up Humanity 15

I   New Thinking.. 21

1   Conscience: More Than Just "Me".................... 22

2   Finding the Bright Side of Globalization 31

II New Actions 43

3   Seeing the World Through Google Earth 44

4   A New Discovery: War Is Futile....................... 66

5   If the Taxpayers Ever Revolted 88

6   The Environment:
    New Planetary Management 109

7   The United Nations:
    Conscience, Not Enforcer 131

III New Challenges... 153

8   The Global Conscience of Religion................. 154

9   Alliance, Not Clash, of Civilizations 175

Conclusion:
Of Conscience, Critical Mass and Hope................. 195

Chapter Notes 199

Index.. 208

Global Conscience at Work

Human Rights Watch 32
International Criminal Court.. 38
Amnesty International 42
Search for Common Ground 47
Global Security Institute 50
Middle Powers Initiative 53
Peace Boat.. 58
Global Action to Prevent War...................................... 70
Institute for Multi-Track Diplomacy 75
Global Youth Action Network....................................... 79
International Campaign to Ban Landmines 85
Grameen Bank.. 92
Pro Mujer.. 94
Project Ploughshares 97
Human Development Report 101
World Hunger Year 105
Parliamentarians for Global Action 112
Parliamentary Network for Nuclear Disarmament......... 118
PeaceJam 123
Building Resources Across Communities 127
United Nations Peacekeeping 136
World Federation of UN Associations 141
Abolition 2000 148
Inter-Faith Action for Peace in Africa........................... 161
Faithful Security 164
Pax Christi 170
Transparency International... 178
Burma Watch International 184
Women in Black... 188
WITNESS... 191

Acknowledgements

The idea for this book came to me on a transatlantic flight to Europe. As I quietly read through a file of reports, UN documents and magazine articles, I suddenly began to focus on the words "global conscience" to encapsulate streams of ideas and activities shoring up the pillars of human security: development, disarmament, environmental protection and human rights. Much creative work is overshadowed by the clouds of war. A new global conscience is being formed, and it needs to be written about.

I wrote a few key words on a sheet of paper and, on my return to Canada, went to see Michael O'Hearn, publisher, and Kevin Burns, commissioning editor, at Novalis. I explained my idea and they said yes instantly. The meeting lasted 15 minutes. One year to the day later, I handed Kevin the manuscript.

This is my third book with Novalis, and I have grown to appreciate the confidence they repose in me. In my conversations with Kevin Burns, I always feel him drawing out the best in me. Anne Louise Mahoney consistently manages the book production with calm efficiency. With her deft copy-editing, Amy Heron greatly improves the clarity of my language. It is reassuring to be backed up by such a strong editorial team.

I received guidance from several individuals. Donna Meen, Director of Library Services at St. Joseph's College, University of Alberta, helped me to find the material I needed on the wide-ranging subject of conscience. Shamil Idriss, executive director of the Alliance of Civilizations

High-level Group, shared wonderful insights into the whole concept of an alliance of civilizations. Bob Miller, director of the Parliamentary Centre, Ottawa, critiqued my thinking, as did Lawrence Martin, author and *Globe and Mail* columnist. Jonathan Dean, of the Union of Concerned Scientists, provided me with valuable material on Global Action to Prevent War. Peter Weiss, a distinguished international lawyer in New York, shared insights on globalization.

Steve Davis, a graduate student at the University of Western Ontario, acted as my research assistant. He did an outstanding job of researching and preparing draft material on the vignettes on organizations reflecting global conscience. His fact-checking work was excellent.

The entire manuscript was read by Bishop Remi De Roo and Peter Mann, whose criticisms and comments enabled me to improve the book. I am deeply grateful to both for the time they took to help me. Remaining errors are my responsibility.

As he has done with my two most recent books, *The Human Right to Peace* and *Beyond Hiroshima*, Khalid Yaqub has prepared a PowerPoint presentation, which I have given to several audiences even before publication of the book. Teachers especially have been responding positively to the visual presentation of the themes in *Global Conscience*. Khalid also maintains my website: www.douglasroche.ca.

It is a joy to once again thank Bonnie Payne for her diligent preparation of the manuscript with its several revisions.

I also want to thank my wife, Patricia McGoey, for her constant support through the writing process.

Douglas Roche
Edmonton, Alberta
March 12, 2007

Foreword

by Roméo Dallaire

Douglas Roche is a true gift to humanity and the peace movement. Over the course of 35 years, the four-time member of the Canadian Parliament and former senator has applied his wisdom, passion and inveterate optimism to the cause of making the world a better place. I would argue that in the pages that follow he has crafted an extremely significant book which marks the apogee of his vision.

He has carefully assembled a novel combination of insights and evidence from disparate fields into a beautiful, holistic concept: a "global conscience" is emerging quite palpably in the world. When one first encounters this observation, one is filled with an overwhelming sense of recognition, for it is something we all know to be true on an intuitive level. However, there is new power to be derived from the very formulation of this perceptible truth, from which we can take hope and begin to envisage possible solutions to the ills of the world.

With great erudition and devotion, Senator Roche has painstakingly collected evidence of this emerging phenomenon, which is breathtaking in its breadth of vision and scope. Amidst a sea of negativity and cynicism about the human condition and the state of the world, this book emerges as a beacon of hope and demonstrates a clear way forward. It is only through our collective recognition of our common humanity and our willingness to respect all human rights that a realistic future is possible.

The emergence of a global conscience is an indication that humanity has evolved to a new stage. We must now ensure that our actions are consistent with this new understanding. Nations often choose to resolve conflicts through indiscriminate violence. The fact that this is the way people have settled disputes historically is an illogical rationale for continued use. It is time that humanity grew up. Just as corporal punishment is not an acceptable way of disciplining children, violence and physical aggression are not an acceptable way of resolving disputes between nations. It is a truism that carrots are almost always more effective than sticks. War and violence can be sanctioned only as the very last resort to avoid massive abuses of human rights such as war crimes, "ethnic cleansing," crimes against humanity and genocide. With hope and a new world order, we can aspire to a time when peace prevails because the root causes have been eliminated.

Until that time arises, the United Nations has enshrined our moral duty to protect each other in its adoption of "the responsibility to protect" ("R2P"), which constitutes an unprecedented recognition of our interconnectedness. In 2005, 191 states made an international commitment to prevent and respond to serious humanitarian crises wherever they may occur. We no longer have the luxury of looking the other way when genocide is occurring outside our national borders, for we are each other's keepers. To look the other way is to violate our moral obligation to each other; to fail to act when one has the resources to help is to sin by omission. Yet, tragically – even with the political legitimacy conferred by the "right to protect" – without political will, genocides continue in plain sight, such as that occurring in Darfur. There is still a reprehensible disconnect between our global conscience and our global actions. It is the challenge of this generation to bridge this untenable gap.

Particularly close to my heart is the topic of global security and human rights. Threats to a sustainable future must be addressed in a human rights context. In keeping with our newfound global conscience, we must formulate a new concept of global security. No single country, no matter how powerful, is capable of going it alone. We are all inherently interconnected and interdependent. Due to this fact, problems cannot continue to be analyzed adequately and solved in isolation. The global situation must be examined in order to achieve a permanent solution. One cannot successfully deal with issues of security without addressing the core problems of poverty, rights abuses, disease, inadequate international development, limited access to education and employment, gender inequality, et cetera. Common sense tells us that throwing billions upon billions of dollars into the maintenance and modernization of nuclear weapons only serves to make us less secure, and diverts scarce global resources away from answering basic human needs which, if ignored, do threaten our global security. We live in a world of hyper-specialization. It is only by going beyond compartmentalization and piecemeal solutions to the examination of the big picture that we shall be able to derive holistic, permanent solutions. When problems that threaten humanity are trans-national in nature, they can be addressed only by looking beyond national borders to the realm of international co-operation.

It is imperative that we realize that we are all in the same leaky boat together. What will save us, if it can only be harnessed, is the will of the people, which historically surpasses that of their leaders in generosity, vision and willingness to change. With unprecedented communication technology, each of you who reads this book has the ability to engage in participatory democracy and make a real difference, should you so choose. Just look at what we hope is a marvellous success story in the making – our awakening to environmental issues such as global warming – which is now proceeding to the next stage of implementing change. We need to use the example of public awareness of environmental problems as a template for other issues of equal and related concern, such as nuclear weapons, poverty, disease and international development.

Senator Roche has chartered a course for us to show us the way forward. Let us have the collective wisdom and courage to embark upon that journey to a hopeful future without delay, for time is not on our side.

Lieutenant General the Honourable Roméo A. Dallaire, O.C., C.M.M., G.O.C, M.S.C., C.D., (Retired), Senator, has had a distinguished career in the Canadian military. *Shake Hands with the Devil: The Failure of Humanity in Rwanda,* his book on his experiences as commander of the United Nations Assistance Mission for Rwanda (UNAMIR), was awarded the Governor General's Literary Award for Non-Fiction in 2004. It has also garnered numerous international literary awards.

As a champion of human rights, Senator Dallaire's activities have included public speaking on issues relating to human rights and genocide prevention; membership in the United Nations Secretary General's Advisory Committee on Genocide Prevention; and leadership in activities aimed at the elimination of nuclear weapons.

Introduction

Lifting Up Humanity

Already the 21st century looks like a repeat of the 20th: every day brings more news of war, poverty, human rights violations and destruction of the environment. This is discouraging, to be sure. But beyond the headlines, something is happening to lift up humanity. An awakening of concern about how we human beings treat one another and the planet is taking place that has tremendous possibilities for moving the world forward to a new era of peace. In fact, this new awareness of a global conscience is the great untold story of our time.

I want to tell this story because it stems from my two most recent books, *The Human Right to Peace* and *Beyond Hiroshima*. The first discusses the ideas for a new culture of peace, as advanced by the United Nations; the second makes the case for the elimination of nuclear weapons as a precondition of peace in the 21st century. The reason there has been any advance at all towards a culture of peace and curtailing nuclear weapons is that a new view of the human being, you and me, is coming into focus at the centre of public policy. A new caring for the wholeness of life is being defined. Humanity is learning to understand all our human relationships, our relationship with the Earth, and how to govern for the common good. This is the stirring of a global conscience.

Wait a minute, I hear you say. Wars are still being fought. Poverty is rampant throughout the developing countries. The air and waters are being despoiled. The most egregious violations of human rights are taking place. Greed and corruption continue to infect political processes. How can I talk about this new maturation of civilization when we are still being dragged down by the same old problems?

That's my first point. We have to be able to see past the problems of the day to observe a shift in human thinking. Many people are calling for a new global ethic to make the world a more human place. The point I want to develop in this book is that a new ethic *is actually being formulated*; I give many examples throughout the book. They are reasons for hope.

Years of lecturing to audiences, and looking into the faces of countless men and women, especially of young people, have taught me that most people want to hear a reason to hope that human security can be achieved. They want to believe that social justice is possible. While it is true that a culture of fear surrounds us—turning many to cynicism and rendering others immobile—I urge readers to take a longer view.

Start with the familiar. We can see a new caring attitude in the spread of anti-smoking laws, campaigns to stop drinking and driving, and measures to cut down noise. New societal concern to provide access to buildings for people with physical disabilities, new efforts to educate people with developmental disabilities, and a drive to stop the exploitation of children are all hallmarks of greater outreach to ensure the well-being of others.

Assembling the evidence of the march of humanity forward reveals an appealing picture. This not only provides hope, but it is also empowering. We feel a new strength to say, "Yes, I can make a difference." It does not necessarily make today's problems go away, but it does help to put these obstacles into perspective and gives us a sense of enlightenment.

Here are a few examples of how I see the stirring of a global conscience.

In the spring of 1963, US President John F. Kennedy, detecting some improvement in US-Soviet relations, made a speech about peace. On June 10, he went to American University in Washington, D.C., and called for a practical peace, "based not on a sudden revolution in human nature but on the gradual evolution in human institutions." He challenged his listeners to look anew at the Soviet Union and the Cold War, to put past conflicts behind them and to concentrate on the common interests of both powers. Then Kennedy spoke words that reached to the core of every culture:

> If we cannot now end our differences, at least we can help make the world safe for diversity. For, in the final analysis, our most basic common link is the fact that we all inhabit this planet. We all breathe the same air. We all cherish our children's future. And we are all mortal.

Kennedy's adversary, President Nikita Khrushchev of the Soviet Union, called it "the greatest speech by any American President since Roosevelt." The speech led directly to the Limited Test Ban Treaty, in which the US and the Soviet Union outlawed nuclear tests in the atmosphere, in outer space and under water.

On December 7, 1988, I was present in the United Nations General Assembly when Mikhail Gorbachev, President of the Soviet Union, astounded delegates when he rejected war as a means of resolving conflicts and called for world policy determined by the priority of the values of all humanity. "The world community must learn to shape and direct the process in such a way as to preserve civilization, to make it safe for all and more pleasant for normal life," he said. Then he renounced force and the threat of force as instruments of foreign policy and said this applied above all to nuclear arms. Gorbachev went on to pledge unilateral troop reductions and drastic cuts in the Soviet military presence in Eastern Europe and along the Chinese border—a move that ultimately allowed Soviet republics to choose their own paths.

Gorbachev's appearance at the UN was the centrepiece of a series of speeches he gave during that period that revolved around his theme: "Today, further world progress is only possible through a search for universal human consensus as we move forward to a new world order." He called for a multilateral centre to lessen the danger of war, a UN verification agency, a world space agency, a world tribunal on terrorism and a special fund for humanitarian co-operation.

There is a common note in Kennedy's and Gorbachev's remarkable speeches: the world is one place and all humanity is interlocked in common survival. Acknowledging this is the first step towards global awareness, which is itself the precursor of global conscience. Neither Kennedy nor Gorbachev was able to implement his vision: Kennedy was assassinated a few months after his speech; Gorbachev was deposed in the implosion of the Soviet Union after the fall of the Berlin Wall in 1989. Few political leaders since (Vaclav Havel of the Czech Republic stands out among this small group) have articulated with such magnetic prose the essence of holistic security, but the political system as a whole is taking halting steps towards interdependence.

The contradictions of globalization are everywhere: stupendous wealth for some, massive poverty for others; freedom for some, subjugation for others; the building of law, and lawlessness. While these contradictions have always been present, they have been exacerbated by globalization. The world now appears to be moving simultaneously in two directions. When terrorists struck on September 11,

2001, efforts to develop a culture of peace were initially put aside in the new "war on terror." But revulsion of war and more violence could not be held down for long and is again quietly being asserted. The millions who marched in cities around the world prior to the 2003 US invasion of Iraq showed the shift in public thinking against war, opposition that has grown each year.

Despite the world disorder, governments and social movements sometimes called civil society are becoming more sensitive to human needs. In 2000, the United Nations issued the Millennium Declaration on the fundamental values of freedom, equality, solidarity, tolerance, respect for nature and shared responsibility. The UN also adopted the Millennium Development Goals, setting achievable targets for combatting poverty, hunger, disease, illiteracy, environmental degradation and discrimination against women, and developing a global partnership for development. At an extraordinary meeting, 1,350 representatives of 100 non-governmental organizations (NGOs) from 145 countries later critiqued government failures in many of these areas and called for such specific improvements as a global poverty eradication fund, binding codes of conduct for transnational companies, and tax measures to support the UN and other international institutions. All these ideas have been carried forward in the World Social Forum, an annual gathering of hundreds of thousands of civil society activists.

The struggle for progress is intense, but gains are being made: the Kyoto Protocol on climate change, the treaty banning landmines, the International Criminal Court, UN peacekeeping missions, the Nuclear Non-Proliferation Treaty, the Millennium Development Goals, the spread of democracy, calls for the reform and strengthening of the United Nations. These are early results of the positive movement forward of history and human consciousness.

The most visible example, perhaps the beginning of the awakening of global conscience, is the charter of the United Nations. The preamble is a call to humanity in eloquent, passionate terms:

> We the peoples of the United Nations, determined to save succeeding generations from the scourge of war, which twice in our lifetime has brought untold sorrow to mankind, and to reaffirm faith in fundamental human rights, in the dignity and worth of the human person, in the equal rights of men and women and of nations large and small …

These words inspire us to recognize that human beings are made for more than a nasty, brutish and short existence. We are made to continue the development of God's planet, which technology now reveals to be one unified place where all human beings have the same joys and hopes, griefs and sorrows. Rooted as we are in our own place and daily concerns, it is a challenge to understand the universal nature of human rights. Thanks to the marvels of communication, we can now be instantaneously connected to people and knowledge to help us understand life around the planet.

Out of the suffering, gloom and seemingly perpetual conflict in the world is emerging a new standard by which we judge right and wrong. Our world is being lifted up, often despite us. We are still mired in conflict, but we yearn to break free from the old bonds that have encased us in our private domains. Increasingly, we recognize that colossal miseries may yet lie ahead. Fear often immobilizes us. Apathy drags us down. But failures in building the conditions for peace ought not to obscure our vision of where humanity is heading in the 21st century.

There is growing recognition of the need for common security. Now we need to affirm that the route to that security lies in public policies built on global conscience.

I

New Thinking

1

Conscience:
More Than Just "Me"

Conscience is that mysterious quality in each of us that tells us right from wrong.

That is a clear enough definition on first glance, but, as with many things in life, the detailed examination of experts, particularly theologians, has complicated it. Theologians say that conscience requires reflective knowledge—having some prior knowledge of an action in order to judge whether it is good or bad. They also point out, of course, that God is watching us and that we cannot fool God even when we try to rationalize our choices.

Theological perspectives are certainly important. As human beings, we are not independent operators. That little voice inside us is related to something bigger than ourselves, much bigger. As the Catholic catechism puts it, "Man has in his heart a law inscribed by God ... . His conscience is man's most secret core and his sanctuary. There he is alone with God whose voice echoes in his depths."

So far, so good. But then the going gets a little heavier. To be fully operative, conscience needs to be able to discern, using "prudent judgment," the moral value of concrete acts. This seems, on the surface, to give us some wiggle room to decide whether an act, bad in some circumstances, is tolerable in others, such as when a poor man steals a loaf of bread to feed his hungry children. Most people could resolve this ethical problem without difficulty. But what about when you discover that the grocery store clerk missed a can of peaches when ringing up your purchases so you did not pay for it? Not your mistake, says one part of your conscience; those peaches will stick in your throat if you do not go back and pay for them, says another. These are simple examples, to be sure.

In contrast, killing another human being is wrong. Surely we can all agree on that. Or can we? Killing in war has long been accepted as morally permissible, under the heading of self-defence. But why is the war taking place? Those who start wars usually claim that the conflicts are just. But "just" by whose standards? Historians, psychologists and novelists have all taken a crack at answering these questions. Even St. Paul had his say. In Romans 2:15, he said that conscience is a witness within all people, including pagans. In his advice to the Corinthians and the Romans, Paul said that those who act against their conscience commit sin. Conscience determines the morality of an action. The Gospels expanded on this theme, emphasizing the interior disposition and purity of intention underlying the external action (Matthew 15:7-20 and Luke 11:39-42).

Then there is the matter of the "erroneous conscience." When you do something that you do not know is wrong (even when others do), have you committed a fault? And whose fault is it that you are ignorant in the first place— yours or society's? Does ignorance of God qualify? No Christian can deny that God has given this gift to everyone. Atheists have every bit as much right to claim they are listening to their conscience as Christians do. But where does belief in Christ fit in? The catechism states that ignorance of Christ and the Gospels can be the source of errors in judgment in moral conduct, as can the bad example of others, enslavement to one's passions and a mistaken notion of the autonomy of the conscience. When a person's ignorance really cannot be overcome, any wrong a person commits cannot be imputed to that person. The act remains no less a disorder or evil, but that person cannot be said to be acting against his or her conscience.

Conscience, when looked at in some depth, does seem a bit slippery. To make the concept easier to grasp, theologians speak of the need to have a "well-formed" conscience, one that is upright and truthful and that formulates its judgments according to reason, in conformity with the true good the Creator's wisdom wills.

Put this way, as the church does, it appears that conscience comes under the watchful eye of religion. In fact, in the early church, there was an assumption that, though all human beings have a conscience, only Christians make full use of it and thus please God. It must be said that the religious scholars of the Middle Ages dwelt on conscience in terms of personal morality, in particular sexual morality, although that was not the only manifestation. St. Augustine wrestled with his conscience in this respect; his *Confessions* are far more subtle and nuanced than the oft-quoted, "O Lord, make me pure but not just yet" suggests. The notion of conscience was given much wider application in elaborating a theory of moral judgment. The Franciscans talked about the heart as the source of judgment; the Dominicans, reason. Thomas Aquinas said conscience always orients us to the good. All these thinkers seemed to agree that conscience is not just an occasional voice at important moments, but is the basis of all morally relevant action.

Mostly, conscience was applied to personal acts. However, the royal laws of France and England developed to give increasing social relevance to the notion of moral conscience. Some of the educated in the 12th and 13th centuries began to be aware that they were one people, living together civilly under a supposedly just and Christian king. There was even a period of courtesy in social relations that underlined the shared will to live together in peace. From the sacred, supernatural realm there emerged some understanding of civil relations. The idea of equity was introduced into law. By the 16th century, conscience among Christians had taken on a cultural aspect. People of conscience were considered spiritual, with obligations to their neighbours, and had, most importantly, a rapport with themselves that led them to feel condemned or saved.

The leaders of the Protestant Reformation saw themselves as the defenders of conscience against "the Pope's commandments." Luther recognized his own scrupulous monastic experience in Paul's idea of conscience: freed by grace, living in faith, the Christian receives a good conscience from God. This aligned with the covenant in the Hebrew scriptures, that God can fathom our hearts and that God alone judges us. But if you were safe in God's arms, were you not above pleasing others or worrying about their opinions? Conscience came to be seen as having little or nothing to do with a person's dealings with others, but only with God's opinion and divine forgiveness. Calvin took this further: the business of conscience is not about people but God, and conscience must certainly not be confused with "police." Religious privacy reinforced this idea; sins are remitted by private confession to God, not a fellow human being. Unfortunately, religious conflict between Catholics and Protestants threw the idea of conscience into confusion. Conscience began to be owned by Catholic and Protestant militants, who then waged wars for the sake of it. But whose conscience? It does not seem that God was frequently consulted.

The introduction of the infallibility of the Pope vastly complicated things. It would be one thing for the church to teach faith and doctrine without fear of error. But did this extend to prudential judgments on the efficacy of political systems? Obviously not. Better to hold onto the central truths of right and wrong. Here, the goodness of God could shine through man's perfidy. Let conscience be the voice of God within us: if you knew God, an intuitive moral law animated you. You could have your private dialogue of the soul with God and be saved. It is this depiction of conscience that led to the "I'm all right, Jack" way of thinking of many otherwise devotedly religious people in modern times.

Technology and the opening up of the world through globalization certainly got in the way of the private dialogue with God. This development is the subject of this book. For now, we have to finish with the subject of how Christian arrogance has skewed our understanding of conscience. Leaving aside the Catholic-Protestant disputes, the idea developed through the ages that only Christians take conscience seriously. Hence, Christians had to liberate the "inferior races" from their idolatrous and superstitious consciences, justifying Western colonialism. Outright slavery was but the worst of this oppression. The plight of Africa today can be traced directly to the Western, so-called Christian, states carving up the continent, oblivious to natural tribal lines, to plunder resources. The mantle of extending civilization was a fraud. Vulnerable people were exploited. There was little, if any, respect for the consciences of people in benighted lands.

The Second Vatican Council (1962–1965) tried to correct this arrogance:

> In a wonderful manner conscience reveals that law which is fulfilled by love of God and neighbour. In fidelity to conscience, *Christians are joined to the rest of [humankind] in the search for truth,* and for the genuine solution to the numerous problems which arise in the life of individuals and from social relationships. [emphasis added]

The Council certainly had an expansive view of the church and indeed the world, which it saw as "the theatre" of human history. At the very least, Vatican II enjoined the followers of Christ to have more respect for others.

Conscience Goes Universal

All religious traditions have notions of law and moral judgment, encourage reflection and offer conceptual tools and practical techniques for self-evaluation. The Hindu and Buddhist faiths have very articulate and complex theories of conscience. Islamic law is shot through with moral considerations. In fact, all the major religions teach the essence of a culture of peace: do unto others what you would have done unto you. The Hindu, Jewish, Buddhist and Muslim faiths all teach what Christians call the golden rule.

Christian triumphalism has seldom been displayed so nakedly as in Christian-Muslim relations. The Crusades of the Middle Ages were probably the worst expression of the denigration of Arab culture, but the response of the West to the terrorism of September 11, 2001, shows how little regard there is for the inherent values of the Muslim faith. In Arabic, the root word *slm* means "to be in peace, to be an integral whole." From this root comes *islam*, meaning "to surrender to God's law and thus be an integral whole," and *muslim*, a person who so surrenders. Obedience to God's law is at the heart of Islamic belief. The violence of the 9/11 terrorists can no more be ascribed to Islam than the Catholic-Protestant killings in Ireland can be blamed on Christ.

Of course, extremists within all religions have fomented violence and wars. But if people today connect violence to Islam or Christianity, it is because such violence is inseparable from the narrative of globalization. Religion is part of this narrative, since religious leaders have failed to curtail their own extremists, but violence today is better explained by the political, economic and sociological injustices in the world. If Christians want to continue insisting that conscience is their specialty, they should be challenged to do a better job of explaining why the Christian West has the lion's share of all the nuclear weapons in the world, which are the biggest affront to both God and human conscience the world has ever seen.

Conscience has had a rough ride through history. If we have learned anything, it is that the white-skinned followers of Christ do not have a monopoly on goodness. And goodness entails considerably more than personal sanctity. This brings us to how, in the 20th century, conscience took on a much wider meaning. The United Nations, which can hardly be called a bastion of religion, put a spotlight on conscience when it adopted the Universal Declaration of Human Rights in 1948. The first article says,

> All human beings are born free and equal in dignity and rights. They are endowed with reason and conscience and should act towards one another in a spirit of brotherhood.

The preamble asserts that violations of human rights "have outraged the conscience of mankind"; article 18 stipulates "the right to freedom of thought, conscience and religion." Conscience has moved out of the preserve of religion, although, I hasten to add, religion ought to be the foremost exponent of the universal recognition that every reasonably developed human being is called to be accountable for his or her actions.

One might even argue that the very existence of the Universal Declaration of Human Rights is an expression of global conscience. It is filled with an uplifting of humanity. It has spawned covenants on the civil, political, economic, social and religious rights of all peoples. Numerous commissions have explored how these covenants can be fully implemented. The development of thinking about humanity fostered by the United Nations, although not exclusively, of course, reveals that the old thinking—conscience as religiously guided personal behaviour—is far too limiting for what is actually happening in the modern world. I will deal with this more extensively in chapter 7. The old questions that stemmed from the idea of personal conduct determining a moral life have given way to new questions about the well-being of the citizens of the planet and of the planet itself. It used to be that the only thing we thought much about was ourselves and maybe our relationship with those we came into contact with every day; however, with science and technology and a new understanding of the inherency of human rights, an integration of humanity is occurring. Not only do we know one another across what used to be great divides, but we also know that we need one another for common survival. There is a new caring for the human condition. This is the awakening of the "global conscience."

Paul Martin, the former prime minister of Canada, used the expression "global conscience" at an international meeting on climate change in 2005. Exasperated at the recalcitrance of the United States in resisting stronger government action to protect the environment, Martin exclaimed, "There is such a thing as a global conscience, and now is the time to listen to it." From the ensuing political comment over the subsequent few days, it appeared that the US government did not appreciate the implication that it cares insufficiently for the well-being of the planet. At least Martin's comment was not dismissed as irrelevant. Progress is measured mostly in small ways. As the columnist Lawrence Martin observed, the US used to have such a conscience. The US was "a nation that showed more respect for human rights and international treaties and consensus-building than it does today."

But such a discussion is getting ahead of ourselves. What I want to emphasize here is that neither wars nor acrimony nor the personal greed that leads to conflict can deny, let alone overcome, the rising sense of a global ethic. This ethic of human rights and planetary stewardship stems from the new global conscience. It is certainly not religions that are imposing such an ethic on the world; for the most part, religions are still internally oriented, though the social teaching of some leads some adherents to strive for peace and world harmony.

Just as personal conscience does not depend on religion for its effectiveness, so too global conscience transcends religions. It is deeply moral, but it crosses boundaries and is becoming interwoven in the processes of daily life. Developing a global conscience is far more than an admonition to do better. Global conscience is a reality, even a phenomenon, of the new age in which the planet has become our common home.

2

Finding the Bright Side
of Globalization

If the notion of *conscience* requires a nuanced understanding, *globalization* is even more difficult to grasp, because it contains numerous contradictions. On the surface, it means that the world is coming together, with greater interrelatedness among people. This is the bright side. The word also signifies the destruction of local economies and cultures, and the decimation of the environment. This is the dark side. Given the ambiguities and linguistic ugliness of the term (*globalism* is not much better), I would like to jettison it. However, this book is about global conscience, so we have to understand the many sides of globalization.

Let's start with the polarities. Globalization signifies the integration and fragmentation of the world going on at the same time. It refers to centralization and decentralization occurring simultaneously. For example, the states of Europe have come together in the European Union, but rebellions are fostering divisions in other places, such as Chechnya, Burma, Nepal, Algeria and Iraq. Terrorists, hackers and militia challenge the forces of capitalism and democracy. New norms of humanitarian intervention clash with local concerns over identity. Nuclear weapons are a sharp counterpoint to social humanitarian movements.

Human Rights Watch

www.hrw.org

Human Rights Watch reports on international human rights violations, as defined by the Universal Declaration of Human Rights and other internationally accepted human rights norms. The organization's goal is to draw attention to abuses and to pressure governments and organizations to reform. The list of concerns is long: traffic in small arms, land mines, gay rights, rights of people with AIDS, safety of civilians in war, use of cluster bombs, child labour, child soldiers, street children, genocide, war crimes and crimes against humanity, torture, extrajudicial killings and abductions, legal proceedings against human rights abusers, and human trafficking. Staff members investigate suspicious situations and seek media coverage of them.

Founded in 1978 under the name Helsinki Watch to monitor compliance in the USSR with the Helsinki Accords, the organization grew and created other "watch committees" to investigate abuses in other regions of the world. By 1988, all the committees united.

Human Rights Watch was one of six non-governmental organizations that in 1998 pioneered the Coalition to Stop the Use of Child Soldiers. A representative of the group has also served as co-chair of the International Campaign to Ban Landmines. The organization gives annual grants to writers worldwide who are in financial need and considered to be victims of persecution. It also promotes freedom of religion and the press, and is part of the International Freedom of Expression Exchange, a global network of non-governmental organizations that monitor censorship worldwide.

Throughout the book are found a number of examples of global conscience at work. For the most part, the organizations depicted in these short sketches are international in scope. They illustrate that global conscience is already having a wide impact on the world.

Contradictions abound. Modern medicine performs daily miracles, yet three million people die every year of preventable diseases. Scientists and astronauts explore the universe, yet 130 million children have no access to education. International law and multilateral covenants exist, yet there is widespread contempt for human rights and the rule of law. More people are living longer, healthier, more productive lives than at any time in history, yet for most of humanity, freedom from want and freedom from fear are as elusive as ever.

The most riveting example of the contradictions of globalization is the fact that the rich are getting richer and the poor are getting poorer. The richest two percent of adults own more than half the global household wealth. Corporate investors are thriving, but health protection efforts and work to secure the planet's air, water and climate are all seriously underfunded. Military spending is considerably more than $1 trillion a year, but the rich countries are stingy about providing aid to the poorest. Countries with nuclear weapons spend billions of dollars every year to modernize their arsenals, but invest only a pittance in the development of Africa. Eighteen of that beleaguered continent's 53 countries experienced a decline in living standards between 1990 and 2003.

Who is responsible for these great disparities and injustices? Who controls the agenda under which the finance and trade decisions are made? The answer is that the world's political and financial elites do, just as they have done for hundreds of years in individual nations.

The prospect of a single global economy dominated by corporate giants has become a focal point of globalization. Their creed is the highest return on existing wealth. Because of it, as Frances Moore Lappe, director of the Small Planet Institute, observes, "80 percent of the world's people live in countries where inequality is worsening and 691 billionaires have come to control as much wealth as half the world's people earn in a year." The corporate class argues that its rising tide lifts all boats. And while it is true that there are growing numbers of rich people in poor countries, the shocking figures of poor people in the world that the UN releases year after year and the desperate pleas of UN agencies for funds to alleviate distress and suffering in the hardest hit areas of the world reveal that genuine concern for the poor is a low priority of the corporate rich.

A New Understanding of Humanity

Corporate magnates, who heavily influence the political agenda when not controlling it, may be the focal point of the contradictions of globalization, but economic and social injustices cannot be traced to only one source. The structures of society, the media, the academic institutions, and the professional organizations all play a role. Globalization does not have a single bogeyman.

Nor is globalization all about inequality. Globalization brings the variegated splendour of the diversity of peoples to the forefront and underlines that there is dignity and worth inherent in every human person. The essential human rights of every person are universal, indivisible, interdependent and interrelated. These are the words UN documents use, and they mean that the farmer I know in Kerala, India, is my brother and the woman I know in Bangladesh is my sister. In other words, I must acknowledge that the human rights I claim for myself also belong to every person on earth.

Globalization is not only about money. It is about awakening our minds to the unity of the human family and the attachment of the family to the planet. Globalization is more than an economic, financial and technological process; it also challenges us to preserve and celebrate the rich intellectual and cultural diversity of humankind and civilization. This is the aspect of globalization that lifts up humankind and is every bit as powerful in shaping history as the merchants who transcend national boundaries. The two sides of globalization, the negative and the positive, continue to intertwine. We fail to capture the power of this moment in history if we concentrate only on the negative.

Shortly after the terrorist attacks of September 11, 2001, the United Nations General Assembly took up the question of why a dialogue among civilizations is necessary to advance the positive meaning of globalization. Since much of the world was still in shock from the terrorist acts, and the drums of a new "war on terrorism" were already sounding, not much attention was paid to the two-day debate. But, by looking at what many countries said about the need to improve awareness of common values, we can see the ways in which globalization should lead to alliances, not clashes. I quote excerpts here to show that wisdom transcends national boundaries.

The debate began with a speech by the former president of Iran, Mohammad Khatemi, who said that a dialogue among civilizations would be the antithesis of hate and intolerance and a preventive tool against terrorism.

> The principle of justice, for example, is a masterpiece of both the Bible and the Koran. Holy Scriptures have played an essential role in the history of mankind for overcoming cases of injustice. In fact, one might argue that believing in God remains an empty phrase or even a blasphemy unless it includes the unshakeable insistence on justice, reconciliation and peace.

> Universality should not be mistaken for uniformity. Where uniformity denies diversity, universality is necessarily inclusive. This very forum—the United Nations—is built on universality and on diversity. Universality is no danger to cultural identity. On the contrary, the recognition of, and respect for, plurality is part of the universality that binds us together. It enables us to recognize differences and to consciously remove barriers. It focuses our minds on what is common to

humanity—our shared values, which are embraced by different religions and societies.

The then UN Secretary-General, Kofi Annan, came to the podium next and said that a dialogue among civilizations is humanity's best answer to its worst enemies.

The idea that there is one people in possession of the truth, one answer to the world's ills, or one solution to humanity's needs has done immense harm throughout history. We need to look no further than the composition of this great Assembly to know—as an unmistakable, incontrovertible fact of life—there are many ways of living, many beliefs, many cultures.

All of us have the right to take pride in our particular faith or heritage. But the notion that what is "ours" is necessarily in conflict with what is "theirs" is both false and dangerous. In contrast to what some would suggest, we can love what we are without hating what we are not.

The debate stressed that there are not good civilizations and bad civilizations; rather, all civilizations are complementary and ought to nourish each other. Representatives of countries such as Algeria, China and Burkina Faso said that the peaceful coexistence and the common development of various civilizations could be achieved only through their learning and benefiting from each other on the basis of equality and mutual respect. But there is, unfortunately, little respect today. The representative from Saudi Arabia spoke forcefully:

It is regrettable that there are latent forces in the West that lie in wait for Islam and the Arabs, see in Muslims and Arabs the real antagonists to the spirit of the times and link them to terrorism. They have substituted the so-called green peril—Islam—for the red menace. Some of these tendentious forces claim that the catastrophe in New York and Washington, D.C., is sufficient proof that the theory that the values of conformity, harmony and relative advantage can be globalized does not apply to the Muslim and Arab worlds, which are propelled by hatred of Western values to the extent that some individuals from those worlds are prepared to face death, to inflict great suffering on the innocent and to threaten to destroy Western societies.

Such tendentious individuals ignore the fact that terrorism is an international phenomenon that is not limited to any one nation, race or religion and that it has been present in every culture and nation throughout history. They ignore the fact that the region that they accuse of hatred is the cradle of the divine religions, which taught the world love and tolerance, and whose peoples have made great contributions to human civilization. Terrorism cannot be an Islamic or Arab phenomenon, as some claim to justify their political ends. The liberal and socialist West and the East with its diverse nations and countries have numerous extremist and terrorist movements. Every culture is subject to those who misrepresent it in a biased manner and whose interpretation of it is at great odds with reality, history and truth.

The representative from Mexico warned about the lack of understanding between the Muslim world and the West and that a breakdown in dialogue could lead to confrontation. The speaker from Armenia said that, with human expansion into other parts of the universe looming, the human race can no longer afford to be weakened by cultural, religious and ideological differences; he pleaded for a dialogue among civilizations as a sign of mankind's maturity and an instrument for progress.

International Criminal Court
www.icc-cpi.int

Created in 2003 by the signing of the Rome Statute, an occasion which brought together representatives from 160 nations, the International Criminal Court (ICC) is the most ambitious international legal body ever created. The ICC investigates and prosecutes genocide, crimes against humanity and war crimes. Its primary goal is to stop these crimes from being committed with impunity. Although the ICC has only been functioning for a few years, it is already having an impact on battlefields around the world.

Unlike other bodies of the United Nations, the ICC is not subordinate to the UN Security Council. In addition, the ICC, under its operating principle of "complementarity," seeks to work with existing judicial bodies (unlike ad hoc tribunals) and only intervene when crimes are committed in signatory nations or by citizens of a signatory nation when the country in question is either unwilling or unable to prosecute. The nation, the UN Security Council or the ICC prosecutor may prompt investigations and prosecutions, which greatly reduces the chance that an aggressor will be able to prevent a crime from being prosecuted. Furthermore, the structure of the ICC allows additional flexibility so that trials may be held either in the nation where the crime was committed or in a neutral location. As a result, the ICC is regarded as being a judicial rather than political organization. A commonly cited example of the success of such flexible, multilateral efforts is the Special Court for Sierra Leone.

The lack of engagement in the debate on globalization by the Western nations was both notable and disappointing. Representatives from the US and Canada did speak, but they concentrated on their nations' successes absorbing into their societies people of many cultures. This achievement undoubtedly has its merits, but the West is generally passive and often hostile to treating other cultures, especially Islamic society, as equals. In fact, it is the self-proclaimed superiority of the West that leads to humiliation and anger in other parts of the world.

The representative from the Holy See tried judiciously to reach into both camps:

> It may seem that any particular culture that is taken seriously raises strong and definitive claims to truth: in a sense, each culture may say that its way is the way, to the exclusion of all others. This determination may even seem to give cultures a certain force. Yet such overly simplistic claims have led, and, sadly, continue to lead, to strife and conflict between peoples, not to mention the number of inhuman and barbarous acts against human dignity, dubiously justified in the name of "culture". All cultures must bear some relationship to freedom and truth. Fanaticism and fundamentalism cannot be equated with the search for truth itself.

Globalization's Common Ground

The UN debate, incomplete as it was, was a milestone because it led to the adoption of a resolution aimed at reinforcing the common ground among civilizations as the basis for globalization. The resolution set out these principles:

- faith in fundamental human rights, in the dignity and worth of the human person, in the equal rights of men and women and of nations large and small;

- fulfillment in good faith of the obligations set out in the UN charter and the Universal Declaration of Human Rights;

- respect for fundamental principles of justice and international law;

- recognition of diversified sources of knowledge and cultural diversity as fundamental features of human society and as indispensable and cherished assets for the advancement and material and spiritual welfare of humanity at large;

- recognition of the right of members of all civilizations to preserve and develop their cultural heritage within their own societies;

- commitment to inclusion, co-operation and the search for understanding as the mechanisms for promoting common values; and

- enhancement of participation by all individuals, peoples and nations in local, national and international decision-making processes.

The sponsors of the resolution did not content themselves with just words to describe the kind of world to which globalization should aspire. Their action program called for widespread interaction and exchange among intellectuals, artists, athletes and tourists, and many conferences to promote a dialogue among civilizations. Youth should be heavily involved. Research, scholarship and the full use of communication technologies should be widely promoted.

This work continues around the world, to varying degrees of effectiveness. The High-level Group on the Alliance of Civilizations, whose report I comment on in chapter 9, is a product of the call for dialogue.

Most of the publicity surrounding globalization does seem to be negative. Anti-globalization movements protest every time the G8 meets or delegates of the International Monetary Fund or World Trade Organization gather. The threat of violence is always real, so police staff the barricades. The public mainly sees confrontation and rarely hears the positive message that many protesters try to send out: that another world is possible. Protesters target globalization because it has led to unprecedented corporate wealth, weapons of mass destruction, genetically modified crops, terrorism, crime, climate change, the loss of forests, water pollution and the depletion of ocean fish stocks. Princeton political scientist Richard Falk speaks of this as predatory globalization. But this is only one side of globalization.

New Stark Questions

The UN debate reflects the human values that can counter the greed and exploitation at the core of commercial globalization. These values—justice, equity, stewardship and non-violence—are the catalyst for rising numbers of civil society groups that are confronting the negative side of globalization and reflect a new power of unity through electronic communication. The questions these groups are asking are becoming clearer and starker than ever, because they emerge out of the frustration of knowing what the physical and financial resources of the earth could offer all people, and of recognizing how the rich and powerful have diverted that wealth to themselves.

- Why is there so much starvation when there is so much food in the world?

- Why are we polluting the atmosphere and waters when we have the technology to avoid this?

- Why do we tolerate the existence of nuclear weapons, which threaten to destroy life?

- Why do we have the United Nations and then refuse to empower it to stop wars and end starvation?

These questions emerge out of the new global conscience and challenge the priorities of governments. Governments get away with inferior answers to questions such as these because the challenge is not yet sufficiently strong. And too much of the challenge is towards ending globalization, as if the modernizing of business systems could be curtailed by fiat. The key issue is, as John A. Coleman, SJ, puts it in *Globalization and Catholic Social Thought*, "How do we humanize globalization and make it serve our habitat and humanity?" Working towards a global ethic, desiring one just world system, developing global governance processes, promoting inter-religious dialogue, encouraging environmental concern, and expanding efforts to educate women are all steps towards this humanization.

We need to see globalization in this positive light. Conscience is telling us that it is wrong to let so many people suffer, to tolerate so much war, to despoil the planet so much. We see discord around the world and we want wholeness. That is global conscience at work.

Amnesty International
www.amnesty.org

Amnesty International is a vivid example of a globally aware citizenry taking a positive attitude and simple steps to improve the lives of people in other nations. The organization strives to abolish the death penalty, torture, inhumane treatment, political killing and forced disappearances.

The group's logo, showing a candle emerging from barbed wire, which is inspired by the Chinese proverb "Better to light a candle than curse the darkness," understates the organization's effect on social change. With 1.8 million members, Amnesty is one of the largest public activist groups in the world. It not only receives timely information from media contacts around the world, but also uncovers breaking critical information with its expert investigations. Its network of field specialists and local contacts are essential in determining the facts of reported incidents. It utilizes letter-writing and education programs to address cases ranging from individual situations to country-wide concerns to global problems. The organization has adopted what it calls the "own country rule," which keeps members out of issues within their own state, which reduces the likelihood of them being persecuted by their own governments.

II

New Actions

3

Seeing the World Through Google Earth

To get an idea of what human security means in a glo-balized world, take advantage of modern technology and do what I did. Using your Internet browser, go to Google Earth (http://earth.google.com) and roam the planet. With the press of a button, swoop down on any corner of the globe. Thanks to satellite photography, you can see city streets, cars parked outside houses, countryside, forests and mountains, lakes and rivers. See the commercial buildings, universities, hospitals and places of worship in every part of the world. Feel the interconnectedness of human endeavour. We are accustomed to seeing photos of the earth taken by the astronauts in outer space. We have absorbed the wholeness, even the pristine beauty, of the globe. From that distance, everything about the earth is one. Now, zooming in on individual cities and neighbourhoods, we see the diversity of human life and its similarities. We see how roads, buildings and services support daily existence, not only in our own communities but also in communities thousands of kilometres away. The two perspectives on the earth complement each other: the whole and the individual become one.

I started with my own home. I inserted the address into Google and suddenly I was behind a camera in space flying at incredible speeds, all the while zooming in on North

America, Western Canada, Edmonton, the south side, the Bonnie Doon area and then my own street. There was my house, the park across the street, the church around the corner, the University of Alberta, a mile or so away, the shopping centre where we buy our groceries, the hotel where I swim every day. All the places that are a part of my daily life were there for me—or anybody—to see.

I could not relax in this peaceful setting. I needed to see war-torn areas of the planet. I typed in "Baghdad." The flying camera hurtled eastward, across Canada, the Atlantic Ocean, and Europe and zoomed in on the Middle East. Baghdad came into clear view. I looked down on a bombed palace, the Ibn Sina Hospital and the American Blackhawk helicopter base. Google Earth's photos are not live but are taken in great sweeps across the planet and stitched together. This picture of Baghdad was taken in 2006. I instructed the computer to go to Haifa in northern Israel, at that moment being bombed by Hezbollah. I moved over to Jerusalem. There, in their glory, were the Church of the Holy Sepulchre, the Dome of the Rock, and other magnificent manifestations of man's relationship to God. Perhaps these holy sites were, for the moment, being spared. What about the people in other areas under attack? Television brings us their faces; that is a human enough depiction for us to absorb. But Google Earth shows us the infrastructure that binds all life. Security is one.

I then went to Congo in Africa and to Kashmir on the Indian-Pakistan border to see more war-torn areas. African or Asian, what difference did it make? Everybody needs water, clean air, a dwelling, access to food and medicine. The contours of the land were certainly different, especially when I tilted the picture for a 3-D effect (another technological marvel). Do the people who live in these areas not deserve the same life-support system that I claim?

I decided it was time for a little fun, so I directed the camera to New York City. There was the Beekman Tower

Hotel, up First Avenue from the United Nations, and my favourite restaurant on 49th Street. The neighbourhood shops were visible, and Google even marked the tourist attractions. Finally, I went over to Pennsylvania to visit my friend Jonathan Granoff. I saw his house in a Philadelphia suburb. His car was in the laneway, but there was no sign of Jonathan. Nonetheless, I felt that I had checked up on him. It was time to go home.

Unlike my regular journeys, this one was hassle-free. No airport security; no flight delays and traffic snarls. I had been around the world, not in 80 days but in a few minutes. I felt connected as never before with every other person on the planet. It used to be said that we should think globally and act locally. Now the local and the global are linked. How can you separate them when technology has joined them together? The fusion of local and global is what globalization is all about. And this realization changes our concept of security.

The Discovery of Human Security

This exciting tour of the modern world prepares us to understand that security today is primarily about the protection of *individuals*, not just the defence of the *state* from external threats. This is a huge leap in human understanding that has come about in the past 60 years.

When the United Nations began in 1945, its charter emphasized that peace and security depended on the settlement of international disputes. While it called for international co-operation to solve economic and social problems, the charter's main focus was on developing friendly relations among states. And it made sure that the rights of the state would prevail by denying authorization "to intervene in matters which are essentially within the jurisdiction of any state," which enabled dictators to cover up a host of sins against their own people, free from fear that another state or the UN itself would step in to stop the brutality.

Search for Common Ground
www.sfcg.org

Driven to find things in common between the people of the United States and the Soviet Union, John Marks, who founded Search for Common Ground (SFCG) in 1982, felt conflict could be fundamentally changed if people were able to "understand the differences, act on the commonalities." Now the organization has 300 staff in 16 countries.

SFCG operates projects that use creative tools to encourage co-operation and non-confrontational solutions to problems. These tools range from radio, television, film and print to mediation, facilitation, training, community organizing, sports, drama and music. SFCG is the biggest producer of radio soap operas in the world after the BBC. In countries such as Sierra Leone, SFCG content is enjoyed by 90 percent of the population. Common Ground Productions, the TV and radio production side of SFCG, created Burundi's first independent radio studio, Studio Ijambo, in 1995. Studio Ijambo has been credited with playing a key role in decentralizing the media in Burundi and building local capacity for news coverage.

When the leaders of the world assembled at the UN in September 2005 to commemorate the organization's 60th anniversary, they issued a declaration showing how global conscience had taken hold in the intervening decades. The leaders acknowledged that

> we are living in an interdependent and global world and that many of today's threats recognize no national boundaries, are interlinked and must be tackled at the global, regional and national levels in accordance with the Charter and international law.

We therefore reaffirm our commitment to work towards a security consensus based on the recognition that many threats are interlinked, that development, peace, security and human rights are mutually reinforcing, that no State can best protect itself by acting entirely alone and that all States need an effective and efficient collective security system pursuant to the purpose and principles of the Charter.

The leaders showed growth in political understanding of security today by affirming,

Peace and security, development and human rights are the pillars of the United Nations system and the foundations for collective security and well-being. We recognize that development, peace and security and human rights are interlinked and mutually reinforcing.

Then came a statement declaring that human beings themselves are at the centre of the peace process.

Acknowledging the diversity of the world, we recognize that all cultures and civilizations contribute to the enrichment of humankind. We acknowledge the importance of respect and understanding for religious and cultural diversity throughout the world. In order to promote international peace and security, we commit ourselves to advancing human welfare, freedom and progress everywhere, as well as to encouraging tolerance, respect, dialogue and cooperation among different cultures, civilizations and peoples.

Of course, actually doing all this would require another step forward in political leadership, but the fact that the leaders were able even to agree that sustainable development and human rights are integral parts of the quest for security is a remarkable testimony to human advancement. How to integrate these ideals into the messy business of state sovereignty remains a challenge, as I discuss below. First, let us look at the sequence of events that led to the 60th anniversary declaration.

The new thinking started in 1971 when a UN commission of distinguished world leaders, headed by Lester B. Pearson, former prime minister of Canada and winner of the Nobel Peace Prize, issued the first major political statement to say that peace can be ensured only by overcoming world hunger, mass misery and the vast disparities between rich and poor. The commission's report, *Partners in Development*, called for a co-ordinated international approach to stimulate aid and development policies. The Pearson Commission set a target for developed countries to transfer 0.7 percent of their gross national product to developing countries as official development assistance. The target is still in place, with only Sweden, Norway, Denmark and the Netherlands having reached it.

At the start of the 1980s, another high-level international commission, led by Willy Brandt, former chancellor of West Germany and also a Nobel peace laureate, published a report on international development, *North-South: A Programme for Survival*. The report linked North-South issues to the East-West conflict, noting that reshaping worldwide North-South relations is crucial to the future of humankind and equal in importance to stopping the arms race. The commission proposed a set of measures, including reforms to trade and monetary regulations. Brandt also linked high spending on arms with low spending on programs to alleviate poverty and ill health in the developing countries.

At almost the same time, a commission headed by Swedish prime minister Olof Palme proposed a policy of "common security" stemming from one overriding conviction: in the nuclear age, no nation can achieve true security by itself. "We are convinced that there would be no victors in nuclear war and that the idea of fighting a limited war is dangerous." In short, Palme's commission argued that the concept of common security must replace policies of deterrence. Common security requires an end to the arms race through negotiation, national restraint and a spirit of collective responsibility and mutual confidence. Moreover, this principle of common security applies to economic as well as to military security. The commission drove the point home: "Countries are joined together by economic inter-dependence as well as by the threat of destruction."

Global Security Institute
www.gsinstitute.org

The Global Security Institute, founded in 1999 by US Senator Alan Cranston, has forged a strategically effective team that includes former heads of state and government, distinguished diplomats, effective politicians, committed celebrities, religious leaders, Nobel peace laureates and concerned citizens. This team works to achieve incremental steps that will enhance security and lead to the global elimination of nuclear weapons. GSI stands for multilateralism, the rule of law and the moral unacceptability of nuclear weapons. GSI works in four results-oriented program areas that target the following:

- heads of government, diplomats and other officials around the world;
- members of the US Congress and their staffs;
- legislators around the world; and
- leaders in the global community.

By leveraging a multidisciplinary approach to policy development by high-level decision makers, GSI continues to make visible contributions to international co-operation and security.

This interdependence became the focal point for a UN expert study on the relationship between disarmament and development, headed by Inga Thorsson, who was then

Sweden's under-secretary of state. The study concluded as follows: "The world has a choice. It can continue to pursue the arms race or it can move with deliberate speed towards a more sustainable economic and political order. It cannot do both." By taking a broader approach to the problem of security, the Thorsson group defined a "dynamic triangular relationship" between disarmament, development and security. The group's report led to the 1987 UN Conference on the Relationship Between Disarmament and Development, attended by 150 nations. (The US refused to attend, stating it did not believe such a relationship exists.) Many countries wanted a special disarmament fund for development, but the attendees, in order to hold Western support, resisted this, contenting themselves with advocating a peace dividend that would result from countries allocating a portion of the resources released through disarmament to economic and social development. But in emphasizing that security consists of "not only military but also political, economic, social, humanitarian and human rights and ecological experts," the conference set the stage for the Security Council's affirmation in 1992 of this very connection. Thus, just at the time the Cold War was coming to an end, a spotlight was put on an overarching fact of security in the modern world: achieving global security is a multi-faceted process involving economic and social development as well as arms control measures, the advancement of human rights and environmental protection, and an end to racial discrimination.

Another prime minister, Gro Harlem Brundtland of Norway, weighed in with a report calling for multilateral solutions to environmental problems through a restructured international system of co-operation. After Olof Palme was assassinated in 1986, the members of the Palme Commission re-assembled in honour of their fallen leader and appealed to world leaders to transform the concept of common security as a protest against war into a comprehensive approach to world peace, social justice, economic development and environmental protection.

The September 11 Derailing

This forward-minded thinking had set the 1990s up to be a period of rejuvenation of peaceful conditions in the world; in fact, the fall of the Berlin Wall in 1989 appeared to be a breakthrough moment. But Iraq's invasion of Kuwait, which led to the first Gulf War, along with anarchy in Somalia, the Yugoslav war, the Kosovo crisis, and NATO's long bombardment of Serbia and Kosovo, combined to jettison the thought of peace dividends as the world focused once more on war as the route to peace. In 1995, another group of world leaders, headed by Ingvar Carlsson, former prime minister of Sweden, and Shridath Ramphal, former secretary-general of the Commonwealth, tried to discourage countries from resorting to militarism as the solution to security problems by promoting the idea of global governance.

> We believe that all humanity could uphold the core values of respect for life, liberty, justice and equity, mutual respect, caring and integrity.

Global governance does not mean global government, Carlsson and Ramphal pointed out. "The challenge is to strike the balance in such a way that the management of global affairs is responsive to the interests of all people in a sustainable future that is guided by basic human values, and that it makes global organization conform to the reality of global diversity"—in other words, global co-operation for the common good.

Prospects began to improve as world leaders gathered at the UN to mark the millennium in 2000. It seemed possible to turn away from militarism and give peace processes some breathing room. The UN advanced the idea of a culture of peace and even declared the first decade of the new millennium to be the International Decade for a Culture of Peace and Non-Violence for the Children of the World. Then the terrorism of September 11, 2001, struck and the budding ideas of a culture of peace were trampled by the re-emergence of the culture of war. The bombing of Afghanistan and Iraq, the US invasion of Iraq, continuing African war crises, more terrorist bombings in London, Madrid and Asia, and the eruption of the Israeli-Hezbollah conflict have dominated the headlines.

Middle Powers Initiative
www.middlepowers.org

The Middle Powers Initiative (MPI), co-sponsored by seven non-governmental organizations with expertise in nuclear disarmament issues, works with "middle power" governments to use their access to nuclear weapons states to fulfill their legal obligations to negotiate nuclear disarmament. MPI focuses on advancing a program of practical steps.

Middle power nations are states that have considerable economic and political power, and a good reputation, and have chosen to forgo nuclear weapons in the pursuit of security. By leveraging this political credibility and material capability, middle power nations can advance compelling discussions with nuclear weapons states. Since its inception in 1998, MPI has sent delegations to Australia, Belgium, Canada, Germany, Greece, Ireland, Italy, Japan, Mexico, the Netherlands, New Zealand, Norway and Sweden, thus engaging governments directly to better inform them about nuclear disarmament strategies. MPI has also hosted several special consultations with governments on topics related to Article VI of the Nuclear Non-Proliferation Treaty in New York, The Hague, Ottawa and Vienna, with 30 states participating.

Nonetheless, as the United Nations prepared to observe its 60th anniversary in 2005, Kofi Annan, by this time himself a possessor of the Nobel Peace Prize, established the High-level Panel on Threats, Challenges and Change, comprising 16 prominent world figures, to assess current threats to international peace and security, evaluate existing policies and recommend ways to strengthen the UN's ability to provide collective security for the 21st century. The panel was chaired by Anand Panyarachun, former prime minister of Thailand, and included Brent Scowcroft, national security adviser to the first president Bush, Yevgeny Primakov, former prime minister of Russia, former prime minister Brundtland of Norway, and David Hannay, former British ambassador to the UN.

The work of the international commissions of the previous decades is evident throughout the panel's report.[1]

The language is urgent in tone and attention grabbing.

- We are approaching a point at which the erosion of the non-proliferation regime could become irreversible and result in a cascade of proliferation …

- International response to HIV/AIDS was shockingly slow and remains shamefully ill-sourced …

- The principle of non-intervention in internal affairs cannot be used to protect genocidal acts of large-scale violations of international humanitarian law or large-scale ethnic cleansing.

The panel found that international security today is threatened by six clusters of threats: economic and social threats, including poverty, infectious disease and environmental degradation; inter-state conflict; internal atrocities; nuclear, radiological, chemical and biological weapons; terrorism; and transnational organized crime.

---

[1]   *A More Secure World: Our Shared Responsibility,* Report of the Secretary-General's High-level Panel on Threats, Challenges and Change (www.un.org/secureworld/).

Though not easy to find, there are non-violent responses to these threats. They lie in a new approach that brings humanity together in common cause.

> What is needed today is nothing less than a new consensus between alliances that are frayed, between wealthy nations and poor, and among peoples mired in mis-trust across an apparently widening cultural abyss. The essence of that consensus is simple: we all share responsibility for each other's security. And the test of that consensus will be action.

When the panel stated, "Many people believe that what passes for collective security today is simply a system for protecting the rich and powerful," that surely was an assertion of global conscience. But it can be rightly asked: where was the global conscience during the Rwandan crisis of 1994, when the slaughter of innocent people amounted to the equivalent of three September 11 attacks every day for 100 days? Why was the international community so silent and the Security Council so dysfunctional during the genocide? Global conscience is still far from a driving force in the resolution of conflict.

When Peaceful Prevention Fails

The panel built the case for a broader understanding of collective security on three pillars: today's threats recognize no national boundaries; no state, no matter how powerful, is invulnerable to modern threats; it cannot be assumed that every state is always able or willing to protect its own people.

Threats today are interrelated. Global economic integration means that a major terrorist attack anywhere in the developed world would have devastating consequences for the well-being of millions of people in the developing world. Already, international terrorist recruitment is aided by grievances nurtured by poverty, foreign occupation and the absence of human rights and democracy, by religious and other intolerance and by civil violence. Poverty, infectious disease, environmental degradation and war feed one another in a deadly cycle. Thus, preventing mass-casualty terrorism requires a deep engagement to strengthen collective security systems, ameliorate poverty, combat extremism, end the grievances that flow from war, and fight organized crime.

Preventive diplomacy to avoid crises was called for as far back as 1992, when former UN secretary-general Boutros Boutros-Ghali issued *An Agenda for Peace*. But time after time, governments have shown either reluctance or disdain for action prior to crises, seemingly preferring to wait until a problem erupts and then going in to pick up the pieces. In pointing to the challenge of prevention, the panel gave first priority to the process of societal development, "because it is the indispensable foundation for a collective security system." Development combats the poverty, infectious disease and environmental degradation that kill millions and threaten human security. Development should be part of a long-term strategy for preventing civil war and addressing the environments in which both terrorism and organized crime flourish.

The panel broke new ground when it wrestled with the question of what happens when peaceful prevention fails. It sought a formula for the use of force within the confines of the UN charter, setting out five guidelines—criteria of legitimacy—for the Security Council to address when considering the use of force.

> Seriousness of threat. Is the threatened harm to the state sufficiently clear and serious to justify the use of military force? In the case of internal threats to human security, does it involve genocide and other large-scale killing?

Proper purpose. Is it clear that the primary purpose of the proposed military action is to halt or avert the threat in question?

Last resort. Has every non-military option for meeting the threat in question been explored?

Proportional means. Are the scale, duration and intensity of the proposed military action the minimum necessary to meet the threat in question?

Balance of consequences. Is there a reasonable chance of the military action being successful in meeting the threat in question, with the consequences of the action not likely to be worse than the consequences of inaction?

Citing these criteria led the panel to call for the right of an ordinary person to be protected against violence:

We endorse the emerging norm that there is a collective international responsibility to protect, exercisable by the Security Council authorizing military intervention as a last resort, in the event of genocide and other large-scale killing, ethnic cleansing or serious violations of international humanitarian law which sovereign Governments have proved powerless or unwilling to prevent.

The "responsibility to protect," a notion that the government of Canada had previously spearheaded through an international commission that built the case for a "right of humanitarian intervention," was thus given prominent endorsement. The panel said that developed states have particular responsibilities to protect vulnerable peoples and should do more to transform their existing force capacities into suitable counterparts for peace operations. The panel also proposed a peace-building commission and a human rights council.

Peace Boat

www.peaceboat.org

Travel to learn about peace. That's the idea behind Peace Boat, an international non-profit organization that works to advance peace, human rights and environmentally sustainable development. Based in Japan, a finely appointed ship regularly journeys around the world. En route, passengers participate in global educational programs, responsible travel, co-operative projects and advocacy activities. This is done co-operatively with other civil society groups in Japan, other parts of Asia and elsewhere.

Peace Boat began in 1983 when a group of Japanese university students felt compelled to do something to address Japan's past military aggression in Asia. The students chartered a boat to travel to nearby countries to learn about World War II. They felt it essential to hear the stories of those who were affected by the Japanese military directly. The organizers of Peace Boat see travel in itself as a potential tool for beneficial social and political change, and seek to create and implement best practices in responsible travel, in what is called "travel for peace and sustainability." By creating partnerships with organizations at the given destinations, Peace Boat believes it can enhance the educational experience. The vessel creates a neutral space that allows people to interact across borders in dialogue and mutual co-operation. This can happen both at sea and in port. In 2006, an American Peace Boat project was created to merge with the Hague Appeal for Peace project.

Following the panel's report, Secretary-General Annan presented his own report, *In Larger Freedom*, drawing on "my own conscience and convictions" to guide countries as to what should be emphasized at the 60th anniversary. The notion of larger freedom, he said, "encapsulates the idea that development, security and human rights go hand in hand." The reinforcing nature of these themes needs to be strengthened in the new era of rapid technological advances, increasing economic interdependence, globalization and dramatic geopolitical change, he said. "We will not enjoy development without security, we will not enjoy security without development, and we will not enjoy either without respect for human rights."

In 2000, the UN had set out a series of time-bound targets for development, ranging from halving extreme poverty to putting all children into primary school by 2015, that were later crystallized as the Millennium Development Goals. The eight goals are to eradicate extreme poverty and hunger; to achieve universal primary education; to promote gender equality and empower women; to reduce child mortality; to improve maternal health; to combat HIV/AIDS, malaria and other diseases; to ensure environmental sustainability; and to develop a global partnership for development. Achieving these goals requires global development assistance to more than double over the next few years. But the performance of the developed countries has not yet matched their rhetoric. That failure, Annan noted in his report, "is measured in the rolls of the dead—and on it are written millions of new names each year." He called specifically for an international finance body to drive the development process in the poorest countries by achieving the 0.7 percent official development assistance target by no later than 2015.

Page after page of Annan's report calls for the international community to take action on a dozen fronts, such as investment priorities, debt, trade, environmental sustainability, science and technology for development, and a comprehensive strategy to end global terrorism—all designed to implement a new security consensus. "We must respond to HIV/AIDS as robustly as we do to terrorism and to poverty as effectively as we do to proliferation." On this last subject, the spread of nuclear weapons, Annan told the nuclear weapons states that they have a "unique responsibility" to further reduce their nuclear arsenals and make such cuts irreversible. Echoing the High-level Panel, he also called for an intergovernmental peacebuilding commission and a new human rights council. One could scarcely ask for more uplifting leadership from the secretary-general of the United Nations.

Unfortunately, the secretary-general does not have a magic wand to make his wishes come true. When the diplomats, for the most part acting on instructions from their capitals, started reviewing a draft outcome document for the 60th anniversary summit, the struggle was intense to get agreement on the proposals of the High-level Panel and Annan's report. Just when agreement was near, the then new US ambassador, John Bolton, arrived on the scene. He had failed to receive confirmation from the US Senate, but the Bush administration used a technicality to give him a recess appointment. Known for his confrontational tactics in diminishing the UN's role in building peace and security, Bolton struck out many passages in the draft. Intense negotiations went on, nearly around the clock. In the process, because Bolton insisted on excising passages calling on the nuclear weapons states to fulfill their disarmament responsibilities, a number of non-aligned states balked at the call to stop proliferation of nuclear weapons, especially by tightening regulations concerning access to nuclear fuels for civilian purposes. In the stalemate, and with the summit about to open, every reference to nuclear weapons was cut from the draft, leaving the world leaders in the ludicrous position of issuing a comprehensive document on peace and security devoid of a single reference to the biggest security threat by far: the 27,000 nuclear weapons possessed by eight states, along with the prospect of more states joining them and the possibility of weapons of mass destruction falling into the hands of terrorists. Annan called the deletion "a real disgrace."[2]

---

[2]   After the Democrats regained control of the US Congress in the 2006 elections and signalled that Bolton would not be confirmed, he resigned.

The US rejection of the Anti-Personnel Landmines Treaty, the International Criminal Court and the Kyoto Protocol, their rescinding of commitments made to the Non-Proliferation Treaty and other diminishments of international law have all undermined the effectiveness of the UN. US unilateralism in invoking war on Iraq greatly destabilized the already precarious conditions in the Middle East. The US is not alone in flaunting international law, but, because of its enormous and unprecedented military power, and its confrontational diplomatic tactics, its actions have a significant impact on the present international system.

A Heightened Sense of Responsibility

The good things that do get done for peace and security are buried in the back pages of newspapers, when they are reported at all. The UN's 60th anniversary summit document was one such good thing. Weakened and timid to be sure, the document, approved by 150 leaders, boosted understanding among world leaders of the interrelated economic, social and military elements of human security. This is global conscience in action in the political arena. While governments are rightly criticized for holding civilization back from developing structures to ensure human security, at least the leaders have changed their vision from that of the old days, when a nation's military strength was the only thing that mattered for security.

When they addressed the new "responsibility to protect" theme, the leaders showed a heightened sense of responsibility for oppressed peoples, even if they did so in general terms. They said that each state has the responsibility to protect its populations from genocide, war crimes, ethnic cleansing and crimes against humanity. In turn, the international community, through the UN, has the responsibility to use appropriate diplomatic, humanitarian and other peaceful means to help protect populations from these crimes.

... We are prepared to take collective action, in a timely and decisive manner, through the Security Council, in accordance with the Charter, including Chapter VII, on a case-by-case basis and in cooperation with relevant regional organizations as appropriate, should peaceful means be inadequate and national authorities are manifestly failing to protect their populations from genocide, war crimes, ethnic cleansing and crimes against humanity.

This document set a new international norm. For the first time, the international community may challenge a state condoning or at least not stopping catastrophic human rights violations, and the state may no longer claim immunity from intervention based on long-standing principles of national sovereignty. Implementing this will be a real test of states' commitment to saving lives. The High-level Panel's five criteria of legitimacy need to evolve into Security Council principles. Since the five permanent members of the Security Council jealously guard their veto power, obtaining agreement for action on a range of issues will be difficult. Does the "responsibility to protect" principle justify the military intervention in Iraq or Afghanistan? Or was this a misuse of it to disguise non-protective military motives? What about Lebanon? Would an invasion of Darfur to stop killings be productive or not?

Some cases are clear-cut and cry out for international intervention. Almost two million people lost their lives under Pol Pot's brutal Khmer Rouge regime during the Cambodian genocide, from 1975 to 1979. In Srebrenica in 1995, UN peacekeepers stood by while Serbian forces systematically selected and slaughtered nearly 8,000 men and boys between the ages of 12 and 60; this was later declared genocide. In Rwanda in 1994, the Rwandan armed forces and Interahamwe militia began the systematic killing of Tutsis and moderate Hutus; approximately 800,000 people were killed in less than four months. The deployment of

UN troops was delayed by disagreements between the US and the UN over the financing of the operation. The UN's 1999 Independent Inquiry on Rwanda concluded that the failure to stop the genocide was a failure of the UN system as a whole, due to the "persistent lack of political will" by member states. These are just a few cases of how the "responsibility to protect," had it been implemented, would have saved many lives.

It has taken horrendous genocides to wake up the world. Lieutenant General Roméo Dallaire, who served in Rwanda in 1993 as a UN Force Commander, has written a searing account of the mass murders of people abandoned by the world's major powers in a vortex of civil war and genocide.[3] The Rwanda story, he wrote, "is the story of the failure of humanity to heed a call for help from an endangered people."

> In the 21st century, we cannot afford to tolerate a single failed state, ruled by ruthless and self-serving dictators, arming and brainwashing a generation of potential warriors to export mayhem and terror around the world. Rwanda was a warning to us all of what lies in store if we continue to ignore human rights, human security and abject poverty.

To protect humanity, Dallaire believes, the UN and its member nations must undergo "a renaissance" and mobilize the political will to act when mass murders loom. The creation of a United Nations emergency police force to prevent genocide and crimes against humanity is essential. But many states fear such an entity on the grounds that it would erode their national sovereignty. At present, the most the UN can do is assemble ad hoc military forces composed of national units or contract the work out to an organization such as NATO. Annan expressed the present dilemma

---

[3]   Roméo Dallaire, *Shake Hands with the Devil: The Failure of Humanity in Rwanda*, Vintage Canada, 2003.

pointedly: "Every time there is a fire, we must first discuss the fire, then find fire engines, and the funds to run them before we can start dousing the flames."

Carrying out the responsibility to protect does not necessarily require military intervention. The peaceful means of conflict resolution, such as mediation and economic sanctions, need to be vigorously pursued. Military intervention to protect people should be a last resort, when all peaceful means of conflict resolution are inadequate. Whether the UN will ever agree to set up a permanent peace-making military force is still an open question.

Agreement on when the international community should jointly use military force to stop killings will require intense diplomatic and political work. This, in turn, requires much more public understanding of the principle of "responsibility to protect" to press governments to join action under the aegis of the Security Council. Gareth Evans, former foreign minister of Australia and a member of the High-level Panel, puts the challenge succinctly: "We have to get to the point where, when the next conscience-shocking mass human rights violation comes along, the reflex response, of both governments and publics around the world, is to find reasons to act, not reasons to pretend it is none of our business." Our common humanity demands that the "responsibility to protect" become a permanent item on the global security agenda, not just in principle but also in practice.

The global conscience has been awakened not only in revulsion to crimes against humanity but also in recognition of the common responsibility to avert them. This is the first step to future agreements on the best means to protect vulnerable peoples. Similarly, the international community now understands that far more than the cessation of military hostilities is required to ensure human security. It just has not yet summoned up enough will to implement all the components of the agenda for peace. The global awakening, however, is taking place.

4

A New Discovery: War Is Futile

On February 15, 2003, more than 10 million people in 600 cities and towns around the world marched against the looming war in Iraq. Huge demonstrations, not seen since the Vietnam War, brought out people of all ages, political opinions and cultures. Two million gathered in London; protesters also assembled in New York, San Francisco, Cape Town, Sydney, Dhaka and Bangkok. In France, upwards of 300,000 protesters—many carrying banners proclaiming "Leave us in peace!"—marched through some 60 towns. Berlin's peace march turned out to be five times bigger than police and organizers expected; at its peak, 500,000 people were packed into the Tiergarten, Berlin's central park.

The massive protests did not stop the war, but they were a way for many people to express their awakened feelings against using war as an instrument of peace. Never before had this happened on such a grand scale prior to a war actually starting. As I write, the war is well into its fourth year. The killings have been massive, the suffering brutal, daily life devastated, the Iraqi people torn apart. The rationales for the war—rooting out the weapons of mass destruction Iraq supposedly possessed, and fostering democracy—have been completely discredited. The fighting goes on because a war has been started. The Middle East, always tinder dry, is now an inferno.

The atrocities of war fill the newspapers and television broadcasts. The incessant reporting creates the impression that there is nothing else but war in the world. It certainly cannot be forgotten that the 20th century saw more than 250 wars, including two world wars and the Cold War, with more dead than in all previous wars over the previous two millennia. Moreover, six million people have died in wars since the Cold War ended. It often seems that humanity is fated for war.

But voices against war are mounting, as evidence accumulates that military force can no longer guarantee victory. Iraq is a prime example. So is Afghanistan. The Hezbollah-Israel war of 2006 ended in stalemate after 34 days of indiscriminate killings on both sides.

The still-young 21st century has already made a profound discovery: military force cannot bring security. Certainly, the "war on terror" has proven to be grossly miscalculated as a way to deal with terrorists or insurgents. The lesson that war is the way to peace is proving to be very hard to learn, but more people are learning it. Those who work for building the conditions of peace still have a hard time being heard. Nonetheless, there is evidence of the diminishment of the culture of war. Reliance on violence for conflict resolution is actually lessening.

The report of the UN's High-level Panel on Threats, Challenges and Change notes that there were fewer inter-state wars in the last half of the 20th century than in the first half, despite the quadrupling of the number of states. The ecumenical coalition Project Ploughshares reported that, although the world endured 32 armed conflicts in 26 states in 2004, this was the fewest in the fewest places since 1987. In 2004, there were four fewer armed conflicts and two fewer states involved in war than in 2003. The Weapons of Mass Destruction Commission, headed by the Swedish diplomat Hans Blix, stated in its 2006 report that "while people will always have their ideological and national differences, the vast majority of humanity appears to be seeking the benefits of an increasingly interdependent world and is not rallying to the idea of an inevitable clash of civilizations." In Blix's words, "a nascent globalization of ethics" is arising from international rules on human rights, themselves a codification of values all people hold.

The most striking evidence of all of the trend to fewer wars and fewer deaths comes from the Human Security Centre of the University of British Columbia, whose director, Andrew Mack, was formerly director of the strategic planning unit in UN Secretary-General Annan's office. The Human Security Centre was established in 2002 by former Canadian foreign affairs minister Lloyd Axworthy and began work on its first annual *Human Security Report*, which appeared in 2005. The global media, said Mack, "give front-page coverage to new wars, but mostly ignore the larger number of existing conflicts that quietly ended." The challenge for the Mack team was to make sense of the mass of often conflicting data and analyses of global and regional trends in political violence. He began his report as follows:

> Over the past dozen years, the global security climate has changed in dramatic, positive, but largely unheralded ways. Civil wars, genocide and international crises have all declined sharply. International wars, now only a small minority of all conflicts, have been in steady decline for a much longer period, as have military coups and the average number of people killed per conflict per year.
>
> The wars that dominated the headlines of the 1990s were real—and brutal—enough. But the global media have largely ignored the 100-odd conflicts that have quietly ended since 1988. During this period, more wars stopped than started.

The report stated:

- The number of armed conflicts around the world has declined by more than 40 percent since the early 1990s.

- Between 1991 (the high point for the post–World War II period) and 2004, 28 armed struggles for self-determination started or restarted, while 43 were contained or ended. There were just 25 armed secessionist conflicts under way in 2004, the lowest number since 1976.

- Notwithstanding the horrors of Rwanda, Srebrenica and elsewhere, the number of genocides plummeted by 80 percent between the 1988 high point and 2001.

- International crises, often harbingers of war, declined by more than 70 percent between 1981 and 2001.

- The dollar value of major international arms transfers fell by 33 percent between 1990 and 2003. Global military expenditures and troop numbers declined sharply in the 1990s as well.

- The number of refugees dropped by some 45 percent between 1992 and 2003, as more and more wars came to an end.

- Five out of six regions in the developing world saw a net decrease in core human rights abuses between 1994 and 2003.

In his report, Mack quickly coupled the good news with a warning that the dramatic improvements are no cause for complacency. Wars, as is all too apparent, are still being fought, and the post–Cold War years have been marked by major war-related humanitarian emergencies, gross abuses of human rights, war crimes and ever-deadlier acts of terrorism. The risk of new wars breaking out, or old ones resuming, is very real in the absence of a sustained commitment by the major powers to conflict prevention and post-conflict peace-building. Nonetheless, the progress cannot be gainsaid. The public gets the impression the world is in a spiral of violence because of media attention, he said during the 2006 Hezbollah-Israel war, adding, "The media is driven by wars. If it bleeds, it leads. But they do not pay attention to the wars that come to an end."

Global Action to Prevent War
www.globalactionpw.org

Deadly conflict prevention, peacekeeping and disarmament: this is what a forward-minded group called Global Action to Prevent War concentrates on. It seeks to eliminate the institutional and ideological barriers that prevent the end of deadly conflict and severe human rights violations.

Global Action, composed of a mix of civil society organizations and a few states, has proposed several stages over the next four decades to move the world from an international system based on conflict and power relations to one grounded in law and multilateral institutions. Consecutive developments in prevention of deadly conflict, non-violent methods of conflict resolution, early warning, peacekeeping and peacemaking, transparency and other confidence-building measures, disarmament, and the utilization of criminal law regarding genocide and crimes against humanity are but a few of the approaches that Global Action has elaborated upon. Dealing also with short-term goals, it has been a strong proponent of a conflict prevention committee in the UN General Assembly and a UN emergency peace service, and contributed to the UN Secretary General's High-level Panel on Threats, Challenges and Change in 2004.

Great care should be taken in assessing current trends. While it is true that, Iraq notwithstanding, the number of armed conflicts is shrinking, it is mainly Africa that has benefited. Wars continue in other regions, and international terrorist incidents increased threefold between 2002 and

2005. Also, campaigns of organized violence against civilians have increased by 56 percent since 1989. Mack has also noted that while it is good news that more wars are now ending in negotiated settlements, the negotiating process often extends the life of the war longer than if "victory" were quickly obtained.

The international community's successes in reducing armed conflict have been achieved despite inadequate resources, weak mandates for UN peacekeeping operations and little support from the countries most able to help. The Mack study is also important because it challenges the international community to figure out why some efforts to prevent or mitigate conflict succeed while others fail.

Credit for War Reduction

The United Nations should be at the top of the list of those who deserve credit for reducing the incidence of war. First, the UN played an instrumental role in decolonization. With the demise of colonization, which had been a major driver of warfare around the world, causing 81 wars since 1816, wars of liberation largely ceased. Second, when the Cold War ended, the UN Security Council, suddenly freed of paralysis, began to play the security-enhancing role that its founders had intended. The UN did not act alone. The World Bank, donor states, regional organizations and thousands of non-governmental organizations played important roles. But the UN was central.

UN peacekeepers have undertaken 60 field missions, with the number of missions increasing by 400 percent since the end of the Cold War. In 2006, there were 90,000 UN peacekeepers serving in 18 operations (including 7,500 police personnel and 4,650 civilians). It is dangerous work; 2,247 UN peacekeepers have been killed in the line of duty. In awarding the 1988 Nobel Peace Prize to UN peacekeeping forces, the Nobel committee commended their work for reducing tensions where an armistice has been negotiated but a peace treaty had yet to be established. "The U.N. forces represent the manifest will of the community of nations to achieve peace through negotiations, and the forces have, by their presence, made a decisive contribution towards the initiation of actual peace negotiations."

UN peacekeeping has become much more than a military operation. It assists in reforming justice systems, training police forces and disarming former combatants. In Sierra Leone, the UN mission disarmed 75,000 combatants, including 6,800 child soldiers, and destroyed 42,000 weapons. In East Timor, the UN mission trained women to enter public service. UN peacekeeping, diplomacy by the secretary-general, disputes being remedied at the International Court of Justice, and a strong norm against aggressive war being upheld all furthered the cause of peace. The High-level Panel noted, "Without the United Nations, the post-1985 world would very probably have been a bloodier place." Blix states, "U.N. peacekeeping operations and peace building are playing a crucial role both in preventing hostilities and in restoring peace in places of conflict." One wonders, with almost giddy anticipation, what the UN could do to prevent future wars if the major powers held back using their veto power and really got behind the UN with political muscle and financial resources. Since this is unlikely to happen in the foreseeable future, the world stumbles on from crisis to crisis, each fuelled by the presence of weaponry.

Death by "Small Arms"

Judging by the statements of many leaders, it appears that governments are waking up to the fact that hundreds of thousands of men, women and children are killed every year by what are called "small arms." These include not only handguns but also any weapon that a single person can carry and fire: assault rifles, automatic weapons, hand grenades, landmines, shoulder-launched missiles and small explosives. Reliable estimates put the number of such weapons in the world at 640 million. Small arms kill more people every year than the atomic bombs dropped on Hiroshima and Nagasaki put together. The small arms trade is not subject to a comprehensive global agreement. Instead, there is a patchwork of national export laws, which unscrupulous arms dealers easily circumvent. The small arms trade alone is valued at $4 billion per year, with the five permanent members of the UN Security Council—the US, Russia, the United Kingdom, France and China—being the biggest traders. At least $1 billion of this trade is illicit, which exacerbates conflicts that kill tens of thousands, sparks refugee flows, undermines the rule of law, and spawns, as Annan has put it, "a culture of violence and impunity."

In 2001, a UN conference on small arms stated the need for an arms trade treaty, a binding international agreement to control the weapons trade under international law that would have helped prevent arms exports to destinations where they might have been used for human rights violations. When the time came to implement this idea at a second conference in 2006, Cuba, India, Iran, Israel and Pakistan, among others, blocked the agreement and the meeting ended in acrimony and frustration. For its part, the US delegation, which included prominent members of the gun lobby, affirmed the right of private gun ownership in passionate and constitutional terms.

Despite the opposition of some governments, most European states are willing to join countries in Africa and Latin America in pressing for meaningful control of the global arms trade (the entirety of weaponry), valued at $44 billion a year. Argentina, Australia, Costa Rica, Finland, Japan, Kenya and the United Kingdom jointly proposed a global treaty establishing common international standards for the import, export and transfer of conventional arms. The US alone voted against a 2006 UN resolution to examine the matter; nonetheless, the creation of an arms trade treaty is now on the UN agenda. Getting it approved requires more dexterous political work than hitherto seen.

Progress may well come when the conscience of humanity is further awakened to the fate of the millions of people affected daily by gun violence. The International Action Network for Small Arms (IANSA), a global network of 700 civil society organizations working for controls on the international arms trade, is spearheading the awakening process. IANSA highlights the human dimension of the problem: while it is mostly men who are killed or injured by small arms, it is women who are forced to flee their homes for an uncertain future. Displaced women often face starvation and disease as they struggle to fend for their families. Much of the violence against women in militarized societies and during armed conflict is an extreme manifestation of the discrimination and abuse that women face in peacetime. More guns mean more danger for women.

There are many examples of this, but perhaps none more tragic than in Congo, where war has raged for a decade, killing four million people. As a result of the constant upheavals caused by the conflict, mothers and children get caught in war zones, hospital supplies run short and children die at shockingly high rates. A 2006 UNICEF report described the death toll in Congo as a "tsunami of death every six months." The number of indirect deaths that can be blamed on small arms is often forgotten, as is the significant social disruption that leads to malnutrition, starvation and death from preventable disease.

The odious recruitment of child soldiers, 300,000 of whom are estimated to be fighting in conflicts in more than 30 countries, is an offshoot of the small arms problem. The weight and size of small arms make them easy for children to handle and encourage the use of children as combatants. It is reported that children as young as eight can easily be taught to fire an assault rifle.

Institute for Multi-Track Diplomacy
www.imtd.org

Multi-track diplomacy refers to the official sphere of government (heads of state, ambassadors) working on an issue with unofficial organizations (civil society and activist organizations). By bringing together the official and unofficial spheres, participants seek to transform the traditional framework of peacemaking.

This is the precise goal of the Institute for Multi-Track Diplomacy, created in 1992. Since then, the Institute has initiated and facilitated conflict transformation projects throughout Europe, Asia, Africa and the Middle East. Most recently, it has been working on projects linked to Georgia, Nepal, Zimbabwe, Somalia, Israel and Palestine, Pakistan and Kashmir as well as on issues related to water and peace and including conflict resolution skills in military training. The Institute seeks to facilitate dialogue between various groups to promote structural change enabling long-term, sustainable peace.

The Institute uses social peace-building to develop the human infrastructure required for transforming a conflict-prone situation. Social peace-building works by improving relationships between groups at a personal level, thus changing perceptions and building relationships based on deep-seated shared interests and values. The Institute uses the term conflict transformation to describe its work because of its suggestion of enabling deep-level change at the systemic level. Peace-building through *conflict transformation* is distinguished from conflict resolution, since it creates the tangible and intangible conditions by which a peaceful system can emerge from a conflict-prone atmosphere.

The gun lobby remains strong. Many more innocent people will be killed and maimed before the international community acts with decisiveness to shut off the flow of weaponry around the world. But the tide of indifference to a murderous trade is turning.

Unseen Horrors of Nuclear Warfare

If it takes so much to energize the awakening global conscience to the calamities brought about by small arms, the effects of which can actually be seen, it is much more difficult to focus public attention on the as yet unseen horrors of nuclear warfare. Of course, the devastation of Hiroshima and Nagasaki is clear to anyone who looks in the files of history. But the absence of nuclear warfare since 1945 has removed nuclear catastrophe from the public mind. Moreover, when the Cold War ended, a myth took hold that nuclear weapons problems had evaporated. Nonetheless, many civil society groups are highly knowledgeable about the birth of the Second Nuclear Age, in which the powerful states maintain nuclear weapons not just for deterrence but also to fight wars. Groups such as Abolition 2000 are trying to build public opinion against the continued evil of nuclear weapons. In 2005, 40,000 people marched in an anti-nuclear demonstration in New York. The Article VI Forum, operated by the Middle Powers Initiative, gathers like-minded states to work on a practical agenda for nuclear disarmament and to strengthen their resolve to press the nuclear weapons states to fulfill their legal obligations under the Non-Proliferation Treaty to negotiate the elimination of nuclear weapons.

In the late 1990s, when the campaign to ban landmines hit full stride, the public responded, especially when people saw the photos of children maimed while playing in fields where explosives were buried. One could hear the cries of many to the politicians: "Do something!" But there are few similar outbursts against the 27,000 nuclear weapons in existence, because there are no modern pictures of the human suffering they could cause. Preventive diplomacy can have no higher purpose than to avert a nuclear war, which would cause unimaginable human suffering and a global economic meltdown. Without photos of such a calamity, civil society groups working on this problem are appealing to the conscience of humanity. A guiding light for the Pugwash movement, which won the Nobel Peace Prize in 1995 for its work on nuclear disarmament, are the stirring words of Bertrand Russell and Albert Einstein, two of the great figures of the 20th century: "We appeal, as human beings to human beings: Remember your humanity, and forget the rest."

A rising public demand for nations to get on with negotiations and implement a nuclear weapons convention to ban the production and deployment of all nuclear weapons may take hold at some point. If this happens, it would be because the global conscience on the immorality and illegality of nuclear weapons had been fully awakened.

When speaking about nuclear weapons, former Secretary-General Annan said the world had reached a crossroads. One path could take us to a world in which the proliferation of nuclear weapons is restricted and reversed through trust, dialogue and negotiated agreement. The other path would lead to a world in which more and more states feel obliged to arm themselves with nuclear weapons, increasing the threat of nuclear terrorism.

> The international community seems almost to be sleepwalking down the latter path—not by conscious choice but rather through miscalculation, sterile debate and the paralysis of multilateral mechanisms for confidence-building and conflict resolution.

The Movement away from Militarism

Annan's description of the crossroads applies to the whole question of war itself. We now have the mechanisms to avert and limit war; indeed, progress has been made. But the conflict-resolution processes are still a veneer over the habitual recourse to war, and so wars keep breaking out. Human society has yet to resolve to go down the path to peace with all that that implies: co-operation, dialogue, reconciliation and laws. And yet the movement away from militarism has clearly begun. But we, meaning society as a whole, still lack the wisdom, patience and courage to forthrightly march down the path to peace that the consciences of an increasing number of people tell us we must. We need to believe that peace is possible.

Deadly conflict is not inevitable. That was the principal finding of the 1994 report of the Carnegie Commission on Preventing Deadly Conflict. Also, in 1986, 20 leading biological and social scientists under the auspices of the International Society for Research on Aggression issued the Seville Statement on Violence, which concluded that there is no inherent biological component of our nature that produces violence. Biology does not predestine us to war and violence. Violence on the scale of what we have seen in Bosnia, Rwanda, Somalia, Iraq and Afghanistan does not emerge inexorably from human interaction. War is a product of our culture. A wide range of factors can lead to war: weak, corrupt or collapsed states; illegitimate or repressive regimes; violent discrimination against ethnic groups; religious extremism; lack of resources; and large stores of ammunition.

All these factors surface when tensions mount because society still accepts that, in given conditions, war is necessary. The machinery we have in hand to prevent war—the UN charter, mediation and arbitration techniques, peacekeeping forces—seems inadequate because it is not fully utilized. When it is, the potential for violence can be defused; political, diplomatic, economic and military measures can and do work, but not when they are subjected to veto by a permanent member of the Security Council with a vested interest in the area of concern. Now, however, with the rapid compression of the world through technological advance-ment, population growth and economic interdependence, combined with readily available small arms, it is essential and urgent to find ways to prevent disputes from turning massively violent. The Carnegie Commission called for an international commitment to the concept of prevention, more effective regimes for controlling destructive weaponry, and higher legal standards to prevent war.

Global Youth Action Network
www.youthlink.org

The Global Youth Action Network, an international network of youth-oriented non-governmental organizations working to cultivate global partnerships, facilitates the active participa-tion of youth at the United Nations. The group holds Special Consultative Status in the UN's Economic and Social Council (ECOSOC) and plans the annual Global Youth Service Day.

Global Youth's newsletter reaches more than 10,000 organiza-tions, distributing news, resources and opportunities around the world. In co-operation with TakingITGlobal.org, Global Youth maintains the Internet's biggest and most active community of youth organizers, students, volunteers and activists. It has also partnered with organizations such as the Youth Movement for Democracy, the Global Youth Coalition on HIV/AIDS, Chat the Planet, Global Youth/Global Justice and the Millennium Devel-opment Goal Youth Campaign. This active and broad partnering strategy has dramatically enhanced opportunities for youth to match their interests and abilities to a broad spectrum of ac-tivist causes. Global Youth's dynamic and innovative approach, combined with partner organizations around the world, has visibly improved youth involvement on activist causes.

In short, war and mass violence usually result from delib-erate political decisions. These decisions need to be infused with a culture of peace—an approach to life that seeks to transform a culture that tends towards war and violence into a culture in which dialogue, respect and fairness govern social relations. If, as UNESCO says, war begins in our minds, then peace must begin in our minds, too.

This is the approach taken by Global Action to Prevent War (see box on page 70), a small but groundbreaking group of scholars and activists who believe that "organized violence is learned behaviour." The answer to this learned behaviour "is to change the pattern of learning, to modify the social values that lead to violence, and to make resort to war more difficult through improved prevention and disarmament."

At the heart of the Global Action program is a plan to build up multilateral capacity to keep the peace and reduce national armed forces until a point is reached at which they can defend their own territory but cannot go beyond it. Global Action proposes a two-thirds reduction of the armed forces of the major powers, with proportionately smaller reductions for smaller powers; complete nuclear disarmament; the end of arms production and transfers, except for the limited amount needed for defence; and commitment by all UN member states not to use armed force except for self-defence or for peace enforcement ordered by the Security Council on the basis of the principle of "responsibility to protect." A standing volunteer UN peacekeeping service would be established; there would be rapid response peacekeeping brigades in every region, thus establishing a multilateral authority with the power to stop wars.

This Global Action program carries out the pledge of general and complete disarmament contained in the Non-Proliferation Treaty. The program would shift decision making on international security issues from the big powers to a responsible, accountable and renewable body in which larger states participate but do not have the dominant authority they now possess. The program is truly revolutionary. That it seems so unattainable in today's world does not diminish its value but rather inspires a potential forward movement of humanity. Societal conscience to stop war has to be first awakened before political policies follow.

In fact, conflict prevention processes are growing and are now well established in Europe. The European Union, embracing 25 countries with a population of 450 million, has contributed to the reconciliation and development of Europe for more than half a century. It is a major peace-builder with a common commitment to peace and security. The European Union defines *conflict prevention* as activities undertaken to alleviate tension and prevent the outbreak or recurrence of violent conflict. For several years, it has engaged in conflict prevention through development assistance, economic co-operation and trade policy instruments, social and environmental policies, and political dialogue and mediation.

The European Union's work is strongly supported by the European Centre for Conflict Prevention, a non-governmental organization based in the Netherlands that led the way in developing the Global Partnership for the Prevention of Armed Conflict, a worldwide network promoting peace-building programs. Under its auspices, 900 people from 118 countries gathered in July 2005 at the UN in New York to launch an international civil society movement to prevent armed conflict. This action was a response to Secretary-General Annan's call for civil society to interact with the UN in conflict prevention efforts.

The Global Partnership has had many successes, not least in the Great Lakes region of Africa, which has experienced the slaughters of Rwanda and Congo. Burundi and Kenya have experienced prolonged conflict, and the Sudan and northern Uganda each underwent terrible civil wars. The cost of these conflicts has been unbearable in terms of the resulting poverty, smashed development and exodus of displaced peoples. It became clear to any objective observer that the promotion of peace and human development in the region requires a fundamental shift from overly reactive approaches to conflict to more proactive, preventive approaches. A team of diverse leaders of non-governmental organizations gathered in Nairobi and identified the following elements as necessary to building peace: legitimate democratic institutions; the rule of law and good governance; respect for human rights and fundamental freedoms; peaceful co-existence and tolerance of diversity; pressure to stop all forms of discrimination; fair management of resources, including land and water; and recognition by the state of its responsibility to protect all its people.

To implement these ideas, the team of leaders called on the governments of the region to set up a specialized agency dedicated to peace-building and conflict prevention to continue the work of the Intergovernmental Authority on Development. The community leaders also called for a special fund to support reconstruction in countries emerging from conflict and urged a regional approach to the control of illicit arms, the condemnation of rape as a weapon of war, the criminalization of resource-based conflicts, and other measures to build the rule of law. Although putting these measures in place is not instantly possible, identifying them is a big step forward in alleviating the continuing suffering in Uganda, Sudan (especially Darfur), and Congo, where killings, rape, displacement and abduction, and the heavy involvement of child soldiers have worn down the populations. The very existence of highly informed civil society leaders in the war zones puts pressure on governments to negotiate peace settlements, demobilize their militaries and reintegrate excombatants into society, and launch healing and reconciliation programs.

People Who Turn the Tide

The 2005 New York gathering of the Global Partnership for the Prevention of Armed Conflict established the International Network for Conflict Resolution Education and Peace Education. That was a tangible outcome. But the Global Partnership did perhaps much more in publishing 65 stories about dozens of peace activists around the world that show what dedicated members of civil society are actually doing to turn the tides of violent conflict.[4]

Berak is a tiny village of 350 inhabitants in Slavonia that was caught up in the Yugoslav war of the 1990s. The village came under Serbian control and the Croats fled; 56 people were killed during the fighting or in the village's detention camp. When the war ended and Berak was reintegrated into the Republic of Croatia, the Croats returned. One of them was Dragica Aleksa. Bitterness between the Croats and Serbs lingered and flared up when a Serb was murdered. The village was traumatized again. To stem the violence, the Center for Peace, Non-Violence and Human Rights in Osijek, Croatia, stepped in and began interviewing villagers. Interviewers followed the "active listening" model pioneered by the US organization Rural Southern Voice for Peace, which gives people ample opportunity to tell their stories. Dragica was interviewed. She recalled of her interviewers, "They were interested in my war experience, in my opinion about Berak today, in my ideas to improve life in that sad village."

"Active listening" is based on open-ended questions. The approach advocates providing time for people to openly express their feelings and concerns, to promote common beliefs and hopes. As the interviews went on, "we could feel the tensions and the hate decreasing," said Katarina Kruhonja, director of the project. Workshops were started, and Dragica, feeling some confidence for the first time, opened a dialogue with a Serb woman. Slowly, more people got involved in the community dialogue. After a while, there was sufficient trust to open up the explosive subject of the

---

[4]   *People Building Peace II: Successful Stories of Civil Society,* Paul van Tongeren, Malin Brenk, Marte Hellema and Juliette Verhoeven, eds. (Lynne Rienner Publishers, Inc., Boulder, Co., 2005).

missing Croat bodies. When graves were discovered, giving rise to deep emotions, the situation stayed calm. Dragica went into a milk-processing plant business with a Serb. She became a leader in the community and, in 2005 was one of the 1,000 women from around the world nominated for the Nobel Peace Prize.

Out of the war and chaos in Liberia, a group of women started the Women in Peacebuilding Network (WIPNET) in the region. They defined their work not just as anti-war activism but also as the deconstruction of structural forms of violence in everyday life: systematic violence against women, such as rape, forced prostitution and mutilation. WIPNET developed a training manual to help women play peace-building roles in Nigeria, Guinea-Bissau, Senegal, Gambia and Mali. The group's biggest success was in Liberia, where women organized mass rallies that resulted in the ouster of Charles Taylor, Liberia's president, who was subsequently indicted by the International Criminal Court for mass crimes. Recognizing the contribution of women, the new transitional government appointed WIPNET members to posts with government agencies. WIPNET was hailed for creating awareness among women of their own powers, giving a human face to conflict, exerting pressure on all sides at the peace table, and rising above the fear that had intimidated women in the past. WIPNET found that preserving the psychosocial well-being of women was vital. The women who left their families behind to do peace work were under enormous stress. Many times, they questioned whether anyone was listening. They kept themselves going by telling stories and singing songs and were inspired by the words of the African-American freedom fighter Harriet Tubman: "If you are tired, keep going; if you are hungry, keep going; if you are scared, keep going; if you want a taste of freedom, keep going."

International Campaign to Ban Landmines
www.icbl.org

The International Campaign to Ban Landmines is a partnership of non-governmental organizations working to abolish anti-personnel mines. It was formed in 1992 when six groups—Human Rights Watch, Medico International, Handicap International, Physicians for Human Rights, Vietnam Veterans of America Foundation, and the Mines Advisory Group—decided to co-operate in pursuing the abolition of these mines. The campaign has grown to a network of 1,400 groups, including those working with women, children and veterans, religious groups, and those involved in environment, human rights, arms control, and peace and development in 90 countries. The campaign's greatest success was the Ottawa Treaty, which bans the production and use of anti-personnel mines. The United States, Russia and China have thus far refused to sign the treaty; nonetheless, the organization was awarded the Nobel Peace Prize in 1997.

The campaign and its network of groups continue to be dedicated to a worldwide ban on the use, production, stockpiling and transfer of anti-personnel landmines. They also call for increased resources for humanitarian mine clearance and mine victim assistance programs. The campaign monitors the mine situation in the world (through a network of researchers who produce the annual *Landmine Monitor Report*) and conducts advocacy activities, lobbying for worldwide implementation of the treaty, humanitarian mine action programs geared towards the needs of mine-affected communities, support for landmine survivors, their families and their communities, and a stop to the production, use and transfer of landmines, including by non-state armed groups.

The stories of the Center for Peace in Croatia and the Women in Peacebuilding Network in West Africa are being repeated around the world as ordinary people work to build peace in their own communities.

The Parents Circle-Families Forum is a group of Israelis and Palestinians—family members of people killed in conflict—working for reconciliation. The group set up the Hello Peace phone line that allows ordinary people from both sides of the conflict to talk to each other.

JAMMA, in Burundi, brings together Hutu and Tutsi youth in activities geared towards reconciliation and re-integration.

Before the official ceasefire and peace process in Northern Ireland, the Peace and Reconciliation Group worked behind the scenes to reduce tension between paramilitary groups and security forces, causing a significant drop in violent activities in the area.

In all this activity, the increasing role of women in building the conditions of peace stands out. In government and through civil society, women worldwide are working in the fields of security, governance, justice and reconciliation. Often at great personal risk, they are taking steps to provide early warning of impending violence, reconcile warring parties, create accountable government structures, and promote the health, education and welfare of the most vulnerable peoples. Since the adoption in 2000 of UN Security Council Resolution 1325, which mandates the participation of women and the inclusion of gender perspective in conflict prevention and peace-building, awareness of the role of women in peace and security has grown tremendously. Women are often now the strongest voices for peace, nonviolence and the promotion of human rights in unstable societies.

The development of a structured role for women in the prevention and resolution of conflict is one of the most important and hopeful signs of the rising willingness to turn away from war. The activity of women spearheads the growing global conscience calling out for peace that, in turn, raises up societal norms. It elevates our understanding that peace is not an abstraction but rather is human-centred.

The forces of war may still operate from the commanding heights of power. The war machinery has the money. But even war profiteering is coming under a new challenge, to which I now turn.

5

If the Taxpayers Ever Revolted

The 2005 BBC documentary film *Why We Fight* opens with a black-and-white flashback to US President Dwight Eisenhower giving his televised farewell address from the Oval Office on January 17, 1961.

> In the councils of government, we must guard against the acquisition of unwarranted influence, whether sought or unsought, by the military-industrial complex. The potential for the disastrous rise of misplaced power exists and will persist.

The phrase "military-industrial complex" was born that night and is at the heart of any discussion of the costs of war. The *military-industrial complex* is generally defined as a coalition consisting of the military and industrialists who profit by manufacturing arms and selling them to the government—in short, the arms merchants of the world. They have been the principal drivers behind the acceleration of world military expenditures to $1.1 trillion in 2005, a 34 percent increase from 1996. Eisenhower, a World War II general whose heroic status catapulted him to the White House in 1952, knew what he was talking about. In his final speech, he added,

> We must never let the weight of this combination endanger our liberties or democratic processes. We

should take nothing for granted. Only an alert and knowledgeable citizenry can compel the proper meshing of the huge industrial and military machinery of defense with our peaceful methods and goals, so that security and liberty may prosper together.

His speech was called one of the greatest ever made by an American president. But his warning ran up against a powerful counterforce: war is profitable for those who manufacture the instruments of war. The top 20 companies around the world profiting from arms sales include 13 American ones. The top three most profitable are all American: Lockheed Martin, Boeing and Northrup Grumman. Their profits are immense, far out of scale of normal businesses. William D. Hartung, an internationally recognized expert on the economies of military spending, says that, contrary to initial expectations, the military-industrial complex did not fade away with the end of the Cold War. It reorganized itself and now receives billions of dollars every year in Pentagon contracts.

On issue after issue, from expanding NATO to deploying the Star Wars missile defence system, to rolling back restrictions on arms sales to repressive regimes—the arms industry has launched a concerted lobbying campaign aimed at increasing military spending and arms exports. These incentives are driven by profit and pork barrel politics, not by an objective assessment of how best to defend the United States ... .

While arms merchants operate worldwide and the five permanent members of the UN Security Council control 90 percent of the arms trade, it is the US that must be the focus. It makes 48 percent of all world military expenditures. NATO allies account for 23 percent and the countries the US has labelled the "axis of evil" account for only about 1 percent. When the extra budget costs of the wars in Iraq and Afghanistan are factored in, the US is spending three quarters of a trillion dollars a year on war machinery.

There is no end in sight. The US maintains military bases in 130 countries and the run-up to space weaponry is now starting. For the development and production of nuclear weapons alone, the US spent $5.5 trillion from 1940 to 1996.[5] Stephen I. Schwartz, who did an exhaustive study, *Atomic Audit*, for the Brookings Institute, reported, "The nuclear weapons complex was given a virtual blank check—or blank checkbook—and allowed to spend money with remarkably little fiscal oversight, congressional or otherwise."

Eisenhower would be stunned at the war machine out of control. Earlier in his presidency, he had shown his sensitivity when he said,

> Every gun that is made, every warship launched, every rocket fired, signifies in the final sense a theft from those who hunger and are not fed, those who are cold and are not clothed.

Such thoughts bring a smile to the cynical.

Even though security has now been defined by the UN in human terms, requiring great investments in economic and social development to spread out the benefits of civilization, the military-industrialists' call for ever greater arsenals of arms prevails in public policy. In the case of the US, the defence industry has ensured that contracts are awarded throughout all the states, thus spurring local economies. Politicians benefit from bragging about how they secure jobs for their people. In turn, contactors reward these politicians with campaign contributions. Fred Kaplan, a respected US journalist who writes on defence matters, said one reason for escalating US military expenditures is

---

[5]   The total amount of spending on nuclear weapons by all nuclear weapons states from the beginning of the nuclear age to the present exceeds $12 trillion.

"Congress' tendency to pile on even more money than the military requests in order to swell the payrolls of local arms manufacturers." Powerful congressional committee chairmen fight for high-cost defence programs "in order to retain constituents' contracts." Many have remarked that Eisenhower should have referred to "the military-industrial-congressional complex." The system is mammoth and it is corrupt. When the Bush administration misled the public and Congress about the reasons for starting the Iraq war in 2003 and secured an authorizing vote for a war that was illegal, Congress failed to hold the president to account because so many Congress members are beholden to the military-industrial complex.

The arms merchants trade on fear. There must always be an enemy. Throughout the Cold War, the public was manipulated into thinking that huge nuclear arsenals were necessary for security. When the Cold War ended, military expenditures fell for a while in the early 1990s, but started rising again in the last part of the decade. With 9/11 and the resulting "war on terror," military spending began to increase again. It will only end when enough people stand up and state clearly to politicians, "We're not going to do this anymore."

An Appeal to the Taxpayer

The groundwork for a revolt against the greedy excesses of the military-industrial complex is being laid today. The infusion into civil society thinking that it is wrong to spend astronomical amounts of money on arms in the name of security when the real human security of millions and millions goes unattended is taking place. The consciences of the advocates of equity have clearly been awakened. The military-industrial complex may appear impervious, but when taxpayers finally figure out that they are not only being lied to but also gouged, the stocks of armaments will undergo new scrutiny. When that day comes, the stock in defence industries will not be worth what it is today.

Grameen Bank

www.grameen-info.org/bank

Awarded the Nobel Peace Prize in 2006, the Grameen Bank is a highly successful investment bank with one of the most unusual models. Unlike most banks, it focuses on making small loans to the poor without requiring collateral. The bank's founder, Muhammad Yunus, was motivated during the intense Bangladesh famine in 1974 to offer a small loan to a group of families so that they could produce small items to sell. He was convinced that if these loans could be made to the poor on a large scale they would be empowered to alleviate the intense poverty throughout the country.

The key innovation the Grameen Bank introduced was the notion that impoverished people are reliable borrowers as long as trust networks are leveraged instead of traditional risk management strategies. Furthermore, the Grameen Bank is owned by its impoverished borrowers, who are predominantly female. This system of microcredit has been adopted in 43 other nations. Typically, a loan is issued to a group of five people, who will be denied future loans if any one of them does not repay. This creates a cultural and economic motivation to act responsibly and hence improve the stability of the overall organization. More than 50 percent of Grameen borrowers in Bangladesh have pulled themselves out of acute poverty. With payback rates of more than 98 percent, and 96 percent of loans going to impoverished women who have seldom borrowed from traditional banking institutions, the Grameen Bank is a spectacular example of how poverty can be alleviated.

The appeal to the taxpayer is precisely the approach taken by the National Priorities Project, a US non-partisan education and advocacy group offering citizens and community groups information to help shape federal budget and policy priorities to promote economic and social justice. The organization points out that for every dollar spent on preventive measures—such as ensuring that nuclear materials are secure, no matter where they are located; participating in multilateral diplomatic and peacekeeping operations; and implementing homeland security measures—nine dollars are spent on military operations.

The National Priorities Project contends that it is largely military spending and militarism that keep the US from addressing critical community needs. The organization brings the information down to the local level, showing in graphs how the taxpayers of Chicago pay $6 billion per year towards the military. This means that they are spending $200 million on nuclear weapons, about as much as it would cost to insure every child in the city who lacks health insurance. They spend $346 million per year for Cold War weapons that have nothing to do with terrorist threats, which is enough to build 2,600 housing units and create 1,200 jobs. Chicagoans spend $3 million *per day* to keep the Iraq war going. For this amount, Chicago residents could hire 62,547 teachers or provide health insurance for 400,000 people, or provide 120,000 four-year university scholarships.

The organization points to public opinion polls showing that when the American public clearly knows where its tax dollars are going, it wants the Pentagon cut by one third and the savings invested in education, health care, the environment, job training and international aid. But this opinion is not yet mobilized into a potent political force. As a result, 31 percent of the children of Chicago go on living in poverty. The education of the public to the shameful discordance of public policies—and the money to pay for them—obviously needs to be stepped up. Campaigns to educate the public about the theft of their own money to support the bloated war machine are needed not only in Chicago and every other American city but around the world.

Pro Mujer

www.promujer.org

Struck by the fact that 34 percent of the Bolivian population lived below the poverty line, Lynne Patterson and Carmen Velasco founded Pro Mujer in 1990. Pro Mujer (Spanish for pro woman) provides services to approximately 130,000 people in Argentina, Bolivia, Mexico, Nicaragua and Peru. The organization focuses on supporting some of the poorest women by helping them with financing, health care and business training.

Intrigued by the Grameen Bank's success in microfinance, representatives of Pro Mujer visited the bank to understand the methods being used so that they could apply them to the situation in Bolivia. After starting to provide financing so that poor women would become self-sustaining, Pro Mujer realized that further business training and health support services were essential to breaking the cycle of poverty. Pro Mujer has increased public awareness about these issues, with stories about its work appearing in *The New Yorker* and *The Los Angeles Times*. With great plans for the future, Pro Mujer hopes to double the number of clients it supports by the end of 2007.

Consider the magnitude of human needs around the world. Since 1990, the number of people living in extreme poverty has increased by more than 100 million. In at least 54 countries, average per capita income has declined in the same period. Every year, almost 11 million children die from preventable diseases and more than half a million women die during pregnancy or childbirth. The continent hardest hit by poverty is Africa. Life expectancy is declining; child mortality remains high. In sub-Saharan Africa, the number of people living on less than $1 a day has increased since 1990. When poverty is added to ethnic and regional inequalities, the grievances that stoke civil violence are compounded.

With access to only a quarter of what is spent world-wide for military purposes, poverty in the world could be eradicated. But the link is rarely made, even by development agencies, which consistently shy away from stressing the impact of arms on development. The agencies appeal to the charity of the public to raise money and seldom point to the militarization and flow of arms around the world as a primary cause of the plight of the afflicted. They continue to operate too much with a compartmentalized mind that says war is war and development is development.

One person who exemplifies this mindset is Jeffrey Sachs, the highly respected development economist and one of the authors of the UN's Millennium Development Goals. His book *The End of Poverty* (Penguin, New York, 2005), an otherwise trenchant exploration of the path out of extreme poverty for the world's poorest people, bypasses the effect of the culture of war on the poor. The words *war*, *arms* and *militarism* do not appear in the book's index. The United Nations Development Program similarly treats the subject only sporadically.

Without a doubt, the attitude of the US government is a principal factor in this inhibition. In rejecting the findings of the 1987 UN Conference on the Relationship Between Disarmament and Development, in which it also refused to participate, the US government said, "We continue to believe that disarmament and development are two distinct issues that do not lend themselves to being linked." The military-industrial complex does indeed have deep roots and powerful influence. To combat it, the public's current passive attitude must be energized. The International Peace Bureau, a network of peace organizations around the world, has launched education programs to focus public attention on shifting investment in war preparations to investment in the needs of the poor and the victims of conflict.

The Link Between Disarmament and Development

There is a solid body of professional work to draw on to build a critical mass of public opinion. In 2004, a team of government experts released a report with updated findings from the 1987 UN Conference. It cited the importance of exercising restraint in military expenditure so that monies could be used to eradicate poverty and achieve the Millennium Development Goals. The report led to a UN General Assembly resolution urging the international community to divert money saved by disarmament to economic and social development and to integrate disarmament, humanitarian and development activities into the Millennium Development Goals.

Freeing the world's peoples from fear and want is at the top of the list of the pressing tasks the international community faces. The founders of the UN saw this and wrote into the charter that peace and security should be achieved "with the least diversion for armaments of the world's human and economic resources." Disarmament and development are two of the international community's most important tools for building a world free from want and fear. Disarmament policies defuse tensions and free resources for economic and social progress; development policies promote stability, thereby creating conditions of increased security; increased security results. This is the "dynamic triangular relationship" that the Swedish diplomat Inga Thorsson promoted in the early 1980s, to which I referred in chapter 3. Disarmament and development are two distinct yet mutually reinforcing processes. Their interrelationship is sophisticated and complex. Each should be pursued regardless of the pace of progress of the other, and certainly neither should be made hostage to the other.

Project Ploughshares
www.ploughshares.ca

Founded in 1976 as an agency of the Canadian Council of Churches, Project Ploughshares' vision is inspired by the following biblical verse:

"God shall judge between the nations, and shall decide for many peoples; and they shall beat their swords into ploughshares, and spears into pruning hooks; nation shall not lift up sword against nation; neither shall they learn war any more." (Isaiah 2:4)

This vision has driven Project Ploughshares to give practical expression to God's call upon humanity to achieve peace, reconciliation and non-violence and thus enable justice, freedom and security for all. Project Ploughshares works with churches and related organizations around the world to develop and implement conflict prevention and elimination programs. Project Ploughshares places particular emphasis on diverting and transforming resources currently used for weapons to human development. It seeks to abolish nuclear weapons, reduce military force in conflict, develop measures to control the supply and transfer of arms, and build conditions that allow for sustainable peace.

Governments, however much they may have given lip service to the idea, backed away from implementation. Whatever gains resulted from lower military spending in the early 1990s went principally into debt servicing, the very debt that military spending during the Cold War had exacerbated. Then came new wars and terrorism and the beginning of the ceaseless "war on terror." Nuclear disarmament discussions came to a standstill; military budgets started rising again.

Although it was a decade of relative prosperity, the 1990s witnessed a widening global poverty gap, with enormous wealth concentrated in the hands of a few. Worldwide, the number of people living on less than $1 a day barely changed. Extreme poverty affects one fifth of humankind. Human development indicators, such as hunger, child mortality and primary school enrollment, have worsened in many countries. Economic and social development have been thwarted by violent and internal regional conflicts, massive flows of refugees, failed governments, illegal trafficking in weapons and narcotics, and diseases such as HIV/AIDS.

Nearly all donor nations, the Scandinavian countries and the Netherlands excepted, fall short of the official development assistance target of 0.7 percent of gross national product, yet their military budgets go up. Aid is marginally increasing at the present time, and the UN's 60th anniversary summit document included decisions to create a worldwide warning system for natural disasters; to mobilize new resources for the fight against HIV/AIDS, tuberculosis and malaria; and to improve the UN's Central Emergency Revolving Fund for disaster relief. But the document was devoid of any mention of the deleterious effects of militarism on development, let alone the relationship between disarmament and development. A central passage calls for mobilizing domestic resources for sustainable development through fostering "freedom, peace and security, domestic stability, respect for human rights … and an overall commitment to just and democratic societies." That is doubtless well-meaning, but fails utterly to come to grips with one of the biggest impediments to sustainable development.

While the United States is at least forthright in rejecting the link between disarmament and development, other major governments are covert and have to obfuscate on this issue to fend off those who promote militarism. While these governments go along with good rhetoric, they do not take a lead in explaining to their publics that excessive armaments spending has a negative impact on development and diverts financial, technological and human resources from development objectives. Armaments in themselves may not be the root cause of violence and conflict, but their spread threatens safety and stability, thus discouraging investment and economic development, and perpetuating a cycle of poverty and distress. There are, of course, many non-military threats to security, including economic instability, health crises, environmental degradation and resource scarcity, and gross violations of fundamental human rights. In each case, these threats are worsened by the diversion of public monies to augmenting military capacities. It is a vicious circle. Governments spend money on arms while non-military threats to security increase. The breakdown of the processes of sustainable development creates unrest, tensions and further destabilization that governments respond to with more arms. That is why the convergence of a large number of states weakened by poverty and rising global military expenditures is so disturbing.

The opportunity costs of high military spending should be another focus of the disarmament-development debate. Considering only the direct outlay of money for the military apparatus underestimates the true costs. There are other significant costs attributable to the research, development, production, deployment and maintenance of weapons systems. Also, the continued development of high-tech weaponry engages the talents and work of countless scientists and researchers who would otherwise be engaged in non-military pursuits. The costs to human health are high. The expense of treatment, rehabilitation and long-term care of those injured places a heavy burden on health systems, when such systems exist. Environmental costs are also substantial. Contamination from nuclear waste and accidents, chemical and biological agents, and landmines often devastates the environment and poses significant social, financial and scientific challenges.

It is ironic that destroying weapons and putting verification systems in place are usually calculated as costs of *dis*armament rather than armament itself. Disarmament can be expensive, and base closures and the demobilization and reintegration of forces can have an impact on a state's short-term economic development. It is ludicrous that the cost of disarmament is sometimes used to justify maintaining levels of military expenditure. Seldom do politicians promote a cost-benefit analysis of peace, economic development and human security, which are nearly impossible to quantify in monetary terms.

The highest costs occur when armed conflict erupts. In the short term, these costs include death, injury and trauma, caring for the wounded, destruction of civilian infrastructure, famine, migration, disease and displacement. The long-term cost is prolonged underdevelopment, which affects future generations. Moreover, the international community bears a considerable burden when it is called on to intervene in a conflict or when it offers humanitarian assistance. Sustainable development clearly suffers when a country goes to war.

What does it take for a state to reduce its military expenditures? Assuming it can control the military-industrial complex, which operates in various forms in most countries, a state will reduce its military spending only when it feels secure and can better utilize its security infrastructure. Transparency and confidence-building measures need to be invoked. Reliable data on military expenditure is frequently scarce. That is why countries should more fully subscribe to the UN's relatively new instruments for standardized reporting. Open reporting and demonstrable respect for international treaty obligations are important elements of confidence building. Regional organizations play an important role in building confidence among neighbours.

The 1987 conference promoted the idea of converting arms factories to civilian production. But it is not easy to convert a factory that makes tanks into one that mass produces refrigerators for Africa. Seeing the transformation costs involved, governments have never been enthused. Often, it is more efficient to shut down military industry facilities than to convert them to civilian purposes. However, the costs pile up. Retraining researchers, scientists and engineers for relevant work in the civilian sector has been one of the largest conversion challenges arising since the end of the Cold War. The need for experts with specialized knowledge of weapons of mass destruction is particularly acute, especially in the light of heightened fears of terrorists using such weapons.

Human Development Report
http://hdr.undp.org

Putting people back at the centre of the development debate is the primary objective of the *Human Development Report*. First produced in 1990, the report goes beyond the question of income and assesses the level of people's long-term well-being. This means cultivating ideas that bring about development of the people, by the people and for the people, and emphasizing that the goals of development are choices and freedoms. Although the United Nations Development Programme commissions the report, it is written independently by a team of leading scholars, development practitioners and members of the Human Development Report Office. The report is translated into more than a dozen languages and released in more than 100 countries annually.

Since the first report, four new gauges for measuring human development have been created: the Human Development Index, the Gender-related Development Index, the Gender Empowerment Measure and the Human Poverty Index. Each focuses on one aspect of the development debate, providing groundbreaking analysis and policy recommendations. The reports' messages—and the tools to implement them—have been embraced by people around the world, as evidenced by the publication of national human development reports in more than 120 countries.

Conversion costs are inevitable if disarmament, in any meaningful form, is to take place. This returns us to the question of conflict prevention as a way to minimize the costs of militarism. By preventing conflict, not only do fewer resources go towards armaments, but economic and social development can also advance as stability and confidence are maintained. That said, reducing military expenditure does not automatically mean that the poor of the world will benefit. There must be a conscious decision at the national level to reallocate released resources to development. A global conscience must push this reallocation.

Two Global Leaders

Two outstanding world figures trying to raise the global conscience on disarmament and development are Oscar Arias, president of Costa Rica, and Jayantha Dhanapala, former UN under-secretary-general for disarmament affairs.

Elected president of Costa Rica in 1986, Arias won the 1987 Nobel Peace Prize for leading a peace plan to stop the continued violence in the region. Since the Costa Rica constitution forbade an immediate second term, Arias stepped down in 1990 and used the $1 million proceeds from the Nobel Prize to start the Arias Foundation for Peace and Human Progress. He became a leading sponsor of the Year 2000 Campaign to Redirect World Military Spending to Human Development. In 2006, Arias was re-elected president of Costa Rica and takes pride in leading a country that has been without an army since 1948. Arias states that "for too long, the worlds of development policy and defence policy have been separated by a stone wall."

> Those who distribute development funds must take into account how military spending is diluting the effect of those funds, and those who draw up military budgets must not turn their backs on human suffering.

Arias believes that "military spending represents the single most significant perversion of world-wide priorities known today." Countries building up stocks of arms, whether they are in the midst of war or not, are taking the surest road that exists to perpetuating poverty among their people. The Year 2000 Campaign represented his vision of a global society committed to demilitarization, collective security and human development. The plan called for the UN to promote mutual and dramatic reductions in military forces and spending, and to redirect the savings to programs to spur economic development and meet human needs. It included proposals for a global demilitarization fund and an international arms trade code of conduct, and promoted demilitarization as a necessary component of democracy. Although the campaign had the backing of 73 prominent organizations, it fell victim to the resurgence of militarism following 9/11. Now that the public is beginning to sour on the strategy of war as a means to peace, the time is right to bring back Arias's ideas.

Jayantha Dhanapala, a Sri Lankan diplomat whose distinguished career led to his 2006 candidacy for the position of UN secretary-general, coined the phrase "sustainable disarmament for sustainable development," which he defines as deliberate action by leaders throughout the world to address the needs of development through the reduction and elimination of arms. In other words, extra money for development would not be a by-product of disarmament; rather, leaders would deliberately chart a course for development augmented by savings from disarmament. In order for governments to come around to this way of thinking (which is definitely outside normal political discourse), diverse groups in society, especially key opinion-makers in government, industry, academia, the public interest community and the media, must urge sustainable disarmament. Sustainable disarmament has to be institutionalized; it requires infrastructure. It ought to be a logical objective of good governance.

But how to get sustainable disarmament and sustainable development integrated into government thinking when governments themselves promote arms sales, albeit indirectly, through their business and industrial policies? The UN's 60th anniversary summit document describes the three mutually reinforcing pillars of sustainable development as economic development, social development and environmental protection. Not a word about disarmament. Changing government thinking is a laborious project and not for the faint of heart. A blend of ideals and self-interest is necessary. What ultimately makes disarmament sustainable, Dhanapala says, "are the benefits it brings to people throughout society, the constituencies that develop a stake in maintaining such benefits, and the consistency of such a policy with public ideals." In short, increase the demand for ploughshares and governments will respond.

A New Framework of Values

However, it is unfortunately true that the idea of disarmament as a direct path to development has lost ground in recent years. Other ideas for promoting security through confidence-building, conflict prevention and peacekeeping have gained ground. Increased awareness of the interdependence of security (understood in the human as well as the state sense) and development is resulting in new ideas to promote both. Will this lead to increased use of non-military resources for security in the future? So far in the 21st century the outlook is not favourable, since states are currently boosting military spending in the name of defending and promoting security. The agenda for development, and hence security, is large and expensive: investment, debt, trade, commodities, rural and agricultural issues, gender equality and empowerment of women, science and technology and, not least, meeting the special needs of Africa. The agenda would certainly be facilitated by an influx of excess military spending.

World Hunger Year
www.worldhungeryear.org

World Hunger Year (WHY) seeks to address the root causes of poverty and hunger. WHY was founded in 1975 by the folksinger Harry Chapin, who believed that solutions to these issues could be found at the local level. As a result, WHY advocates long-term solutions by supporting community-focused organizations that enable citizens to be self-sustaining. Job training, after-school programs, housing and health care access, microcredit and entrepreneurial training are examples of these self-sustainability projects.

WHY's areas of work include WHY Speaks, which produces reports on water and food security, globalization and economic justice; an online centre for food security learning; a UN program that reports on sustainable development, the Millennium Development Goals and human rights; and the Global Movements program on the basic rights to food, water, land, jobs, credit, and reform of agriculture and trade policy. WHY believes that hunger and poverty can be ended by changing public views and influencing policy makers.

Global understanding that security requires the implementation of the agenda for development is, of course, a big step forward even when governments are still being squeezed by the tentacles of the military–industrial complex. Governments are now trying to streamline the mechanisms of the old economic system, which puts the individual first and features a top–down approach to the well–being of society. The brutalities of the current system are largely responsible for the unbearable disparities today. There is not much appetite within government, and probably not much in society as a whole, for the implementation of what is called in liberation theology the "preferential option for the poor." This means gearing the economic system around human needs rather than the accumulation of wealth.

If the new ideas of security seen through the prism of human needs are to reach their full blossoming, we need a framework of values that provides guidelines and priorities for structuring society so that human dignity is promoted. In other words, it is not just sustainable development that needs to be pursued, so that there will be some resources left on the planet for future generations, but *equitable* sustainable development. This approach, in the eyes of the defenders of the status quo, gets dangerously near the dreaded redistribution of wealth concepts associated with communism. But social justice principles, which hold that the state should serve the needs of the individual (and not the other way round, as the communists would have it), are very much a basis for fully implementing the human security agenda. Ideas for redistributing wealth, such as a carbon tax or a currency transaction tax, are diametrically opposed to the prevailing ideology of accumulation of individual material wealth, with competition benefiting the strongest and economic growth being the main tool for development.

A progressive system of redistribution of wealth would start with the developed countries giving a time-bound guarantee that the developed countries reach the 0.7 percent of gross national product target for official development assistance (the year 2015 has been proposed), with poverty eradication the overriding objective. A carbon tax and a currency transaction tax,[6] with the proceeds dedicated to sustainable development purposes, have also been proposed,

---

[6]   This would be a tax of perhaps 0.5 percent on all speculative transactions, as first proposed in 1972 by the Nobel Prize–winning economist James Tobin. Huge amounts of money could be raised for sustainable development through such a mechanism.

along with comprehensive debt cancellation programs for the poor countries. These countries should have more representation on the international financial institutions, such as the International Monetary Fund and the World Bank.

The immense and as yet untapped mineral wealth at the bottom of the oceans should benefit sustainable development, not just the fortunate entrepreneurs who get there first. Developing countries must be helped to pay for education and health, priorities that are not susceptible to the demands of the marketplace. Women's increased access to resources, such as land, education and technology, must be fostered. In international relations, the selfish G8 countries—the United States, Japan, Germany, France, the United Kingdom, Italy, Canada and Russia—need to realize that they cannot solve economic, social and security problems themselves, but need to work with other countries such as China, India, Brazil, Mexico and South Africa on the same footing. A G20 has been proposed that would include even more countries. Perhaps, in the name of equity, it would be better to make the United Nations, which already exists, a more effective instrument for ensuring sustainable development.

Sharing power and resources would put some human values into sustainable development. The global partnerships now talked about need to become a reality. The "right to development" has long been proclaimed, but so far lacks the financing to achieve it. Many schemes have been proposed. For example, the UN Development Programme has proposed reducing greenhouse gas emissions through pollution permit trading and cutting poor countries' borrowing costs by securing the debts against the income from stable parts of their economies. A failure of imagination is the least of the sins of the powerful governments who could, if they had values-based policies, lift up the world economics. If they met the Millennium Development Goals by raising their official development assistance of $70 billion in 2006 to $130 billion in 2015, more than 500 million people would be lifted out of poverty, saving millions of lives, giving millions of children an opportunity to attend school, reversing environmental degradation and averting conflict, among other benefits.

With the values of a culture of peace rather than the culture of war driving economies, globalization could indeed take on a permanently attractive face. With world population on its way to 9 billion people, compared to about 6.5 billion now, the demand for energy and other natural resources will grow exponentially, and pressures on the environment may become intolerable or, to put it in modern jargon, unsustainable. What will be the answer then? More troops? The profits of the military-industrial complex, at an all-time high today, may well turn to ashes tomorrow.

6

The Environment:
New Planetary Management

Vanity Fair. National Geographic. Time. These and count-less other popular publications have discovered that environmental protection is newsworthy enough to feature on their covers. The headlines cry out: "Global Warm-ing: A Graver Threat Than Terrorism"; "Global Warming: Bulletins from a Warmer World"; "The Challenge of Climate Change." Google lists 128 million entries containing the phrase *global warming*. Amazon.com lists 917 titles on the subject. "Kyoto" is now understood better as an interna-tional treaty to stop severe climate change than the cultural centre of Japan. Global conscience about the environment has clearly awakened.

One of the most effective prodders of this conscience is former US vice-president Al Gore. In 1992, Gore established his credentials as a passionate defender of the environment with his book *Earth in the Balance,* in which he said, "I cannot stand the thought of leaving my children with a degraded earth and a diminished future." After his unsuccessful run for the presidency, Gore devoted himself almost full time to the climate crisis and developed a slide show to demonstrate the effects of global warming. This led to his bestselling book, *An Inconvenient Truth,* which, in turn, led to the movie of the same title. The movie won an Oscar in 2007 for best documentary. Gore has put the case for protecting the environment before millions of people. Global warming, he says, is "a planetary emergency."

> It is up to us to use our democracy and our God-given ability to reason with one another about our future and make moral choices to change the policies and behaviours that would, if continued, leave a degraded, diminished and hostile planet for our children and grandchildren—and for humankind.

Gore has an easy way of explaining the basic science of global warming. The sun's energy enters the atmosphere in the form of light waves and heats up the earth. Some of that energy warms the earth and then radiates back into space in the form of infrared waves. Under normal conditions, the atmosphere naturally traps a portion of the outgoing infrared radiation, which is good because it keeps the temperature on earth within comfortable bounds. The problem we now face is that this thin layer of atmosphere is being thickened by huge quantities of human-caused carbon dioxide and other greenhouse gases. When we burn fossil fuels (oil, natural gas and coal) in our homes, cars, factories and power plants, or when we cut or burn down forests, carbon dioxide is released into the atmosphere. As the gas thickens, it traps a lot of the infrared radiation that would otherwise escape the atmosphere. As a result, the temperatures of the earth's atmosphere and oceans are getting dangerously warmer.

Global temperatures are shooting up faster than at any other time in the past. Global warming threatens to raise sea levels as much as three feet by the end of this century, due to melting glaciers and swollen oceans. Global warming is also bringing heat waves that are now causing torrid summers in the northern hemisphere and making hurricanes and tornadoes more powerful and more destructive. Major storms in both the Atlantic and Pacific since the 1970s have increased in duration and intensity by about 50 percent. The

World Health Organization estimates that climate change is largely responsible for killing 50,000 people a year, mainly in Africa and Asia.

This is what the climate crisis is all about. According to both the Pentagon's Office of Net Assessment and Sir David King, Britain's chief scientific adviser, it is a far greater threat to the world than international terrorism. Without immediate action, floods, drought, hunger and debilitating diseases such as malaria will hit millions of people around the world. James Hansen, one of the world's most prominent environmental scientists, says the greatest threat of climate change for human beings lies in the potential destabilization of the massive ice sheets in Greenland and Antarctica. The level of the sea throughout the globe is a reflection of changes of global temperature. When the planet cools, ice sheets grow on continents and the sea level falls. Conversely, when the earth warms, ice melts and the sea level rises. Low-lying cities in countries around the world, from Bangladesh to the United States, could be inundated. Any future rise in the sea level will result, dramatically, from the increase in greenhouse gases.

The scientific debate for the responsibility for global warming is over. The scientific community is agreed: it is humans causing this crisis. The landmark 2001 Report of the UN Intergovernmental Panel on Climate Change stated, "There is new and stronger evidence that most of the warming observed over the last 50 years is attributable to human activities." The International Panel issued follow-up reports in 2007 warning of the effects of a warmer world: more extreme temperatures, including heat waves; new wind patterns; worsening drought in some regions, heavier precipitation in others; melting glaciers and Arctic ice; and rising global average sea levels. The Union of Concerned Scientists says scientists can now positively identify the "human fingerprints" left on earth's climate. From 1950 to the present, most of the global warming has been caused by heat-trapping emissions from human activities—burning fossil fuels and clearing forests.

Parliamentarians for Global Action

www.pgaction.org

Parliamentarians for Global Action is a unique network of 1,300 legislators from 114 parliaments engaged in a range of action-oriented initiatives. Concerned parliamentarians from around the world established the non-profit, non-partisan group in 1978 to address global problems that could not be solved by any one government or parliament. Although the organization's initial focus was disarmament and the prevention of nuclear proliferation, it today works on a larger list of worldwide concerns, such as fostering democracy, conflict prevention and management, international law and human rights, population and sustainable development, by informing, convening and mobilizing parliamentarians.

Prime ministers, cabinet ministers, and chairs of parliamentary finance, foreign affairs, population, health and defence committees are but a few of the myriad roles represented. Members have included former presidents of Iceland, Botswana, Trinidad and Tobago, and the Philippines, and former prime ministers of Canada and New Zealand. With a membership of legislators from elected parliaments, usually coming from both governing and opposition parties, members are able to bring a broad spectrum of opinions from their constituents. As a result, the group cultivates connections on policy issues between the executive branches of governments and civil society.

The Development of Agenda 21

Efficient use and conservation of resources to improve living standards were among the United Nations' first concerns. The 1949 UN Scientific Conference on the Conservation and Utilization of Resources brought together for the first time scientists and experts on economic and social development. "No citizen has the right to damage fellow citizens by reckless and wasteful use of resources," they declared. Industrial pollution, management of hazardous wastes, rural–urban migration, the fouling of oceans and seas, and the prospect of climate change were subjects beginnning to be discussed in the 1950s and 1960s. Rachel Carson's *Silent Spring*, published in 1962, sounded the alarm about environmental damage and health risks from excessive use of pesticides and other agricultural chemicals introduced in the 1940s and 1950s.

Developing and industrialized countries were sharply divided on environmental issues. Industrialized countries became concerned with pollution, conservation of genetic and natural resources, and the pressures created by growing populations on resources and energy supplies. Developing countries tended to dismiss environmental concern as the business of rich countries. Their energy and resource consumption were not high; industrial pollution was localized, if present at all. What concerned them were poverty and its effects: short life expectancies, infectious diseases, and inadequate shelter, water and sanitation. These countries were tempted to industrialize by the cheapest route first and fix the resulting pollution problems later, using as a comparative advantage their willingness to accept industries that had become intolerable in the developed world.

A start at reconciling the differences between the industrialized and the developing countries was made at the 1972 UN Conference on the Environment, held in Stockholm. This led to the creation of the UN Environment Programme. In 1992, on the 20th anniversary of the Stockholm conference, 103 heads of state gathered in Rio de Janeiro for the Earth Summit and adopted Agenda 21. This 800-page blueprint of 115 programs dealing with every known environmental ailment was costed at $625 billion. The developing countries said they would pay $500 billion, leaving only $125 billion to be paid by the developed countries. But the rich balked. The document was adopted by consensus only after developing countries dropped their demand for specific commitments for aid from industrialized nations to pay for the plan. New aid from the rich announced at the summit did not amount to much more than $2 billion. Maurice Strong, the indefatigable Canadian who chaired the conference, said that the summit was "a launching pad, not a quick fix." The summit's strength lay in this: it began a new process of planetary management. The gathering of national political leaders, the demands of thousands of highly informed observers from non-governmental organizations, and the impact of the media all widened decision making about planetary development.

The Kyoto Protocol: Not Enough

One of the hard-won agreements at the summit was the Framework Convention on Climate Change, a legally binding treaty to curb emissions of carbon dioxide, methane and other greenhouse gases. In the language of UN documents, "Such a level should be achieved within a time frame sufficient to allow ecosystems to adapt naturally to climate change to ensure that food production is not threatened and to enable economic development to proceed in a sustainable manner." What this meant was good intentions without a time commitment. Virtually all countries, including those of the European Union, wanted a global commitment to reduce carbon dioxide emissions after 2000 to levels lower than those of 1990. The US, by contrast, insisted on no targets and timetables on grounds of cost. At the final preparatory meeting, the US government threatened that then President Bush would not attend the summit unless the target dates were removed. High-ranking officials of the summit later said privately that the price paid to obtain the presence of the US president was too high. Nonetheless, a treaty existed requiring industrialized countries to limit their emissions of greenhouse gases, to protect forests and other systems that absorb these gases and to demonstrate, at a later date, what they have done to reduce emissions to 1990 levels.

That later date proved to be 1997, when the Kyoto Protocol was negotiated, requiring industrial states to reduce greenhouse gas emissions to 5.2 percent below 1990 levels by 2012. Since three quarters of all greenhouse gases are emitted by the United States (30 percent), Canada (2.3 percent) and Europe, including Russia (41.4 percent), the Kyoto Protocol established binding targets for industrialized countries but not for developing ones. The objective was the stabilization of gas emissions to prevent further damage to the atmosphere. A complex formula was included, permitting developed countries to earn emission allowances by investing in sustainable development projects in developing countries. However, even if successful, the Kyoto Protocol would fall far short of stopping the global average rise in temperature of 1.4°C predicted to occur before 2100. Some areas of the planet will see considerably higher temperature rises. When it is remembered that the average temperature of the earth's surface has risen by 0.6°C since record-keeping began in the late 1800s, it is clear that time is running out to solve this problem.

In its 2001 report, the International Panel on Climate Change urged that emissions fall to 60 percent below 1990 levels before 2050, over a period when global population is expected to increase by 37 percent and per capita energy consumption will rise dramatically, as billions of people in the developing countries climb out of poverty. By this measurement, the demand of the Kyoto Protocol is modest, if not too weak, given the magnitude of the problem.

Nations met in Montréal in December 2005 and adopted a number of measures to speed up the implementation of Kyoto, but did not set commitments beyond it. At least a dialogue on strategic approaches for long-term global co-operative action has started.

By 2006, 164 countries had ratified the Kyoto Protocol, accounting for 65 percent of global greenhouse gas emissions. But the US, which has only 5 percent of the world's population but produces 30 percent of global emissions, rejected the treaty; the Bush administration, casting doubt on the scientific evidence, has scorned it and claims that it would cause havoc on the US economy. Global co-operation is further hindered by China and India's refusal to sign the Protocol. China is of particular concern, since it has the second-highest carbon dioxide emissions, with a rapidly developing economy and increasingly high levels of energy use, especially from coal-fired power stations.

It is certain that global warming will continue as long as greenhouse gases increase. Rising seas, fiercer heat, deeper droughts and stronger storms are ahead for humanity, unless greenhouse gas emissions are severely cut.

The Dangers of Nuclear Power

At this point, we must ask ourselves whether nuclear power could be a solution to the global warming crisis. The debate on this subject rages, with proponents claiming it will save the day and opponents maintaining that the risks are unacceptable.

From the dawn of the nuclear age, nuclear technology has been recognized as having two uses. The same nuclear reactors that give bombs the destructive force of many thousands of tons of high explosive can, when harnessed in a controlled fashion, produce energy for peaceful purposes. The challenge is to prevent the proliferation of nuclear weapons while still permitting countries to produce nuclear energy. Atomic energy thus presents an unprecedented challenge to the world. Will it lead to sustainable development or the destruction of the planet?

Already, nuclear science has played a key role in enabling humanitarian benefits essential to development: diagnosing and curing cancer, providing higher yielding, disease-resistant crops, reducing airborne and waterborne pollution, and, not least, producing 16 percent of the world's electricity with almost no greenhouse gas emissions. The nuclear industry contends that the only way the electricity needs of the multiplying billions in the developing world can be met over the next quarter century is through nuclear power. Even conservation measures in the industrialized countries and increased reliance on renewable energy sources would not satisfy the coming demand for energy. In addition to fossil fuels already polluting the atmosphere and causing global warming, two thirds of the world's oil reserves are located in the Middle East, which is constantly vulnerable to political change, resulting in wild fluctuations in the price of oil. Energy needs and environmental degradation will be the supreme security issues of the 21st century, nuclear proponents argue. Since nuclear energy does not add to the greenhouse effect, does not contribute to acid rain and does not deplete the ozone layer, its substantial advantages suggest it could play a far more important role in the future than it does now.

An opposite view holds that nuclear energy creates a legacy of serious and long-lasting environmental and health problems and that it enables proliferation of nuclear weapons. The 1986 accident at Chernobyl released 300 times the radiation let loose by the Hiroshima bomb and contaminated adjoining countries. In addition to health hazards, the problem of safe disposal of radioactive waste for up to 250,000 years is overwhelming. There is no known way of storing this waste safely and securely for a long period. Opponents of nuclear energy hold that it is irresponsible to keep producing this waste before scientists have developed storage methods and tools to communicate information about that waste to future generations, who could overcome these problems.

Parliamentary Network for Nuclear Disarmament
www.gsinstitute.org/pnnd

With more than 500 members, ranging from Argentina to Zimbabwe, the Parliamentary Network for Nuclear Disarmament (PNND) is dedicated to supplying parliamentarians around the world with up-to-date resources on nuclear weapons policies and to helping parliamentarians become involved in nuclear nonproliferation and disarmament activities. It operates as the parliamentary wing of the Middle Powers Initiative (see page 53).

PNND's electronic communications network provides members with the following:

- information on nuclear disarmament issues and on international events, including United Nations disarmament meetings;
- samples of parliamentary resolutions, motions, questions and legislation from around the world;
- contacts with parliamentary colleagues in other countries with whom to share information and ideas;
- a forum for developing joint strategies between parliaments; and
- links with disarmament experts.

Recent successes of PNND include hosting three international conferences, in Strasbourg, Vancouver and Wellington, and organizing cross-party discussions on nuclear weapons policies in the European Parliament and in Belgium, Canada, India, Japan and New Zealand.

The controversy over the wisdom of nuclear power is exacerbated by its potential for misuse. Under the terms of the Non-Proliferation Treaty, countries have an "inalienable right" to research, produce and use nuclear energy for peaceful purposes. They are proscribed from using their access to nuclear technologies to make a nuclear weapon. Yet that is what Iran and North Korea have been charged with doing.

The making of a nuclear weapon is not particularly difficult when the right fuels are present. A nuclear weapon requires either highly enriched uranium or plutonium. Because only a small amount of either substance is needed to build a bomb, terrorists could feasibly steal enough material to build one or more nuclear weapons. While low-grade uranium in many reactors cannot be used for bombs, it can be so used when enriched.

Almost 60 states currently operate or are constructing nuclear reactors, for a total of 440 around the world. At least 40 of these states possess the capability to build nuclear weapons. Collectively, these states have enough highly enriched uranium and plutonium to build more than 100,000 additional nuclear weapons. In 2004, the UN High-level Panel on Threats, Challenges and Change pointed out that, regardless of whether more states acquire nuclear weapons, the existence of large stockpiles of nuclear and radiological materials poses grave risks.

Despite the dangers, energy ministers from many countries are convinced that only by building more nuclear power stations can the world meet its soaring energy needs while averting environmental disaster. China alone intends to build 30 nuclear reactors. In the past, the virtual absence of taxes on greenhouse gas emissions from oil, coal and gas plants has meant that nuclear power's advantage, low emissions, had no tangible economic value. But the Kyoto Protocol requires plant operators to pay for their pollution. Combined with soaring fossil fuel costs, this is persuading countries to intensify nuclear production.

The environmental problem has thus come full circle. The high consumption demands of the rich countries have resulted in intolerable global warming. Global warming threatens the continuation of stable development of the planet, adversely affecting rich and poor together. The rich balk at taking and paying for sufficient steps to curb global warming. Nuclear energy is advocated as a cost-efficient way of providing increased energy. But it compounds the risk of planetary destruction by runaway production of nuclear weapons, which can be stopped only by strict multilateral controls on nuclear fuels, which the major countries oppose for commercial reasons. The pursuit of profit exacerbates the climate crisis and undermines the common good of the planet, including the rich. The rich want to have their cake and eat it, too.

Not the least of the benefits of the Kyoto Protocol was fixing the blame for global warming where it belongs: the industrialized countries. For too long, the population surge, which is occurring overwhelmingly in the developing countries, has been blamed for poverty-worsening pollution. The link between population, poverty and pollution is false. Poverty is frequently the result of the destruction of traditional cultures, of the North's plunder of resources in the name of economic growth, of the uprooting of people who are then left with no choice but to vegetate in the festering slums or devastate the remaining wilderness. In short, it is not populations that cause poverty; rather, it is endemic poverty that stimulates population growth, which can best be curbed by the education and health programs that are part of the Millennium Development Goals. Meanwhile, with the Kyoto Protocol, the developed countries, except the United States, have acknowledged their larger responsibility for the environmental crisis.

Obviously, alternative sources of energy are needed along with more comprehensive energy conservation practices. Renewable energy sources—wind, waves, tides and the sun—all have shown promise for meeting increased energy needs. It is estimated that wind power, which currently comprises less than one half of one percent of the electricity supply, could expand to 15 to 20 percent of that supply with proper infrastructure changes. It is known that harnessing sunlight could power civilization 2,000 times over, but solar power from photovoltaics would increase the cost of electricity by three or four times. It is a false economy to continue to rely so heavily on depleting fossil fuels, which are themselves so vulnerable to wars, but that seems to be the way the world works. The Kyoto Protocol has encouraged the development of renewable energy sources that could gradually correct today's excessive dependency on fossil fuels. And increasing numbers of business innovators are heading down this road. But the world's addiction to oil seems, at least at this moment, incurable. The participants in the UN's 60th anniversary summit agreed to "promote innovation, clean energy and energy efficiency and conservation; improve policy, regulatory and financing frame works; and accelerate the deployment of cleaner technologies." The leaders did not talk about money for this.

There is no hint that world leaders are willing even to think about eliminating nuclear power. In fact, the High-level Panel on Threats, Challenges and Change included nuclear power on its list of energy sources requiring more development. To rely on nuclear power as a "magical fix" for global warming would require the production of many new reactors, posing unacceptable risks of accidents or terrorist attacks. Some estimates indicate that to meet the future demand for electricity through nuclear power alone would require the average of one new reactor to come online somewhere in the world every 15 days between 2010 and 2050. This rate of nuclear development would be irresponsible in the extreme. A 2003 study by the Massachusetts Institute of Technology concluded:

The potential impact on the public from safety or waste management failure and the link to nuclear explosives technology are unique to nuclear energy among energy supply options. These characteristics and the fact that nuclear is more costly, make it impossible today to make a credible case for the immediate expanded use of nuclear power.

Facing Up to the Crisis of Humanity

We are left with a mix of technologies to develop renewable energy plus more rigorous energy conservation measures and full implementation of the Kyoto Protocol as the best hope of containing the global warming threat. Will this combination be enough? The most optimistic answer is maybe. But the political sluggishness all too apparent in today's leaders suggests a less hopeful answer. All but the most obdurate of the group seem to recognize the gravity of the environmental crisis, but cannot muster the will to take the costly action necessary. As for the public, the global conscience on the environment has been awakened, but not yet to the point of seeing that global warming is itself part of a larger problem.

The moral choice society faces is more than whether to use or reject nuclear power as a way to curb global warming or what quantitative target to set to satisfactorily control greenhouse gas emissions. The choice is whether to maintain the current global system, which is overwhelmingly weighted in favour of the developed countries and discriminates against the increasing number of vulnerable people in the developing countries. When the question is framed this way, global warming is clearly a symptom of a much deeper problem. Global warming results from the consumerism that drives the Western economies, a consumerism built for a century and a half on exploitation of resources and wealth by the powerful of the world. A declining minority have aggrandized the lion's share of the world's wealth, polluted the planet, risked the future and deluded themselves that more militarism will successfully counter the growing demands for equity by the increasing majority of the world. This is simply not sustainable. It is not just sustainable development that is at risk. It is sustainable human life on this planet. The crisis of the environment leads us to face up to the crisis of humanity.

PeaceJam

www.peacejam.org

PeaceJam directly changes the lives of thousands of youth around the world every year by getting them working with some of the most inspiring and exciting people who have ever lived: Nobel Peace Prize laureates. These eminent personalities include the Dalai Lama, Archbishop Desmond Tutu and Aung San Suu Kyi. Laureates work with youth so that they may pass on the spirit, skills and wisdom they exemplify. PeaceJam has inspired a new generation of peacemakers to contribute to positive change within themselves, in their local communities and around the world.

Youth draw lessons from laureates' lives, which the youth may directly apply to work on violence and racism. This includes practical techniques for making an enemy into a friend, developing awareness of one's own culture and cultivating a sense of responsibility, family and community. Participants then design and implement a school or neighbourhood service, local or global in scope, that addresses a problem and demonstrates the traits of peacemakers and problem solvers. Each PeaceJam group selects four candidates to attend the annual PeaceJam conference. Proposals are presented at the annual conference and participants meet their peers from around the world.

Al Gore complains that efforts to strengthen laws in the US to curb greenhouse gas emissions have been thwarted by business interests, who have used the same methods as cigarette manufacturers to discredit evidence that smoking is a cause of lung cancer. A few multinational companies have spent millions of dollars to sow public confusion about global warming. "The truth about global warming," Gore says, "is especially inconvenient and unwelcome to some powerful people and companies making enormous sums of money from activities they know full well will have to change dramatically in order to ensure the planet's livability." These business interests have emphasized both uncertainty and the prospect of economic dislocation in an effort to paralyze the political process. These tactics themselves are gradually being discredited, so chances are increasing that the new media blitz on the perils of global warming will result in stronger laws. That is definitely movement forward but still does not address the social and economic divisions and marginalization of the poor that are at the root of the environment crisis.

It is true that climate change issues for the rich are, as Gore notes, "an inconvenience." But for the poor, they are a disaster. In Africa, multiple stressors—the spread of HIV/AIDS, the effects of economic globalization, such as the privatization of resources, and armed conflict—are converging with climate change. The consequences of overgrazed land, deforested mountainsides and denuded agricultural soil mean that nature will be more vulnerable than previously to climate change. Dryland agriculture will produce decreased yields even with only minimal increases in temperature. Such changes are already causing disruptions in food supply in Malawi and Niger. Higher ocean levels are starting to contaminate underground water sources in Israel and Thailand. The people most vulnerable to these changes are those who lack the resources to migrate. They are trapped by their poverty.

Jeffrey Sachs has written in *Scientific American* that small changes in climate "can cause wars, topple governments and crush economies already strained by poverty, corruption and ethnic conflict." A drought-induced famine is much more likely to trigger conflict in a place that is already impoverished and bereft of any cushion of physical or financial resources. The deadly conflict in Darfur, which is almost always discussed in political and military terms, has roots in an ecological crisis directly arising from climate shocks. When the rains faltered in the 1980s, violence ensued as communities fought to survive by raiding others and attempting to seize or protect scarce water and food supplies. Climate change affected the El Niño in 1998, producing huge floods off the coast of Ecuador, which destroyed export crops and aquaculture. That led to a failure of loans to Ecuador's already weak banking system, provoking a bank run, economic collapse and eventually the ouster of the government. Sachs says that climate skeptics who ask impatiently why we should care about "a degree or two" increase in the globe's mean temperature understand neither the climate nor the social and economic systems in which we live. The debate on global warming ought surely to include the ecological effects on societies already facing hunger or financial and political fragility.

The developing countries have a right to a level of economic development that reduces poverty. Poor countries and their peoples ought not be made to bear an undue share of the burden of the global adjustments needed to address climate change. A full response by the developed countries to global warming would include additional official development assistance for sustainable development as well as technological assistance to adopt more benign and efficient energy sources.

Issues of social justice are inextricably woven into the repair of global warming. The test of global conscience will be in how the wealthy minority of the world respond to the dislocation and suffering of the most vulnerable, not just to how the current system of negative globalization can be kept going with the smallest possible adjustment.

The Oxford Research Group, a distinguished group in the UK that specializes in security issues, takes a comprehensive view of the climate crisis and says it can be resolved only with a "sustainable security" strategy. Its 2006 report[7] links climate change, competition for resources, marginalization of the majority of the world's people, and global militarization as the root causes of conflict and insecurity. Washington, London and other Western capitals have falsely projected international terrorism as the greatest threat facing the world.

Interestingly, the risk of further terrorist attacks will increase if these other threats are not dealt with. But current policies in these areas are self-defeating in the long term, and so a new approach is needed.

The Oxford Research Group cites these elements of a new approach to sustainable security, in terms of possible responses to current threats:

- **competition over resources**: comprehensive energy efficiency, recycling and resource conservation and management polices and practices;

- **climate change**: rapid replacement of carbon-based sources by diversified local renewable energy sources as the primary basis of future energy generation, and the worldwide phasing out of civil nuclear power programs;

- **marginalization of the majority world**: reform of global systems of trade, aid and debt relief in order to make poverty reduction a world priority;

- **international terrorism**: addressing the legitimate political grievances and aspirations of marginalized groups, coupled with intelligence-led counter-terrorism police

---

[7]   *Global Responses to Global Threats: Sustainable Security for the 21st Century*, by Chris Abbot, Paul Rogers and John Sloboda, Oxford Research Group (www.oxfordresearchgroup.org.uk).

operations against violent revolutionary groups and dialogue with terrorist leaderships wherever possible; and

- **global militarization**: alongside non-proliferation
  measures, bold, visible and substantial steps by nuclear
  weapons states towards disarmament, while halting vertical
  proliferation initiatives, such as the development of new
  nuclear weapons and new bio-weapons.

Building Resources Across Communities
www.brac.net

Building Resources Across Communities (originally Bangladesh
Rural Advancement Committee, BRAC) is one of the world's largest non-governmental organizations. Created in 1972 by Fazle
Hasan Abed, BRAC began by focusing on small-scale relief and
rehabilitation projects to help war refugees after the Bang-
ladeshi liberation war of 1971. The organization now provides
financing to and leads development activities with 4.8 million
members in 65,000 villages in all 64 regions of Bangladesh,
and does outreach in Afghanistan, Sri Lanka and Africa. BRAC is
76 percent self-financed through its enterprises, which include
microcredit banking, a food project and a network of retail craft
stores. In 2004 Abed was awarded the United Nations Development Programme Mahbub ul Haq Award for his outstanding
contribution to human development.

Recently BRAC has begun to work with people who cannot access microfinance due to extreme poverty, creating a program
specifically for this group that uses subsidies and business
development training, health care, social development and as-
set transfer to eventually raise the ultra poor to the point that
they can use BRAC's primary microfinance service.

Implementing this agenda requires new thinking.
Without it, the security policies of the wealthy countries
will continue to be based on the mistaken assumption that

the status quo can be maintained—that is, that the rich can preserve their security without fundamentally altering the global system that keeps the poor downtrodden. A new vision is needed that addresses the various causes of global insecurity in a coherent way. This is an argument for governments and civil society to link questions of peace with anti-poverty and environmental issues.

Hints of a new integrated approach are contained in the UN's 60th anniversary summit document, but governments are too wary of the opposition of vested interests to take compelling stands. Much more work by civil society is needed to overcome the recalcitrant forces that continually drag down the world. The civil society representatives who work with the governmental representatives on the Commission of Sustainable Development are constantly trying to uplift the vision of governments, but they still resist it. Where new thinking flourishes is in such documents as the Earth Charter.

The idea of a charter to set out principles for achieving sustainable development goes back to the 1980s. It was given new life in 1997 by Maurice Strong, chairman of the Rio Earth Summit, and Mikhail Gorbachev, former president of the Soviet Union. They and a team of experts, working with the input of 5,000 people, agreed to a charter in 2000; over the next five years, 2,400 organizations representing millions of people endorsed it.

> We stand at a critical moment in Earth's history, a time when humanity must choose its future. As the world becomes increasingly interdependent and fragile, the future at once holds great peril and great promise.

The Earth Charter is now recognized as a global plan for sustainable development. It says that the dominant patterns of production and consumption are causing environmental devastation, the depletion of resources and a massive extinction of species. A global partnership to care for the earth must be formed or we risk the destruction of ourselves and the diversity of life. Therefore, we must decide to live with a sense of universal responsibility, identifying ourselves with the whole earth community as well as our local communities. The Earth Charter gets down to business with a list of new norms. Here are just two.

- **Adopt patterns of production, consumption, and reproduction that safeguard Earth's regenerative capacities, human rights, and community well-being.**

    a. Reduce, reuse, and recycle the materials used in production and consumption systems, and ensure that residual waste can be assimilated by ecological systems.

    b. Act with restraint and efficiency when using energy, and rely increasingly on renewable energy sources such as solar and wind.

    c. Promote the development, adoption, and equitable transfer of environmentally sound technologies.

    d. Internalize the full environmental and social costs of goods and services in the selling price, and enable consumers to identify products that meet the highest social and environmental standards.

    e. Ensure universal access to health care that fosters reproductive health and responsible reproduction.

    f. Adopt lifestyles that emphasize the quality of life and material sufficiency in a finite world.

- **Ensure that economic activities and institutions at all levels promote human development in an equitable and sustainable manner.**

    a. Promote the equitable distribution of wealth within nations and among nations.

b. Enhance the intellectual, financial, technical, and social resources of developing nations, and relieve them of onerous international debt.

c. Ensure that all trade supports sustainable resource use, environmental protection, and progressive labor standards.

d. Require multinational corporations and international financial organizations to act transparently in the public good, and hold them accountable for the consequences of their activities.

In the end, the environmental crisis is about consumerism versus stewardship. It is a profound issue of global conscience. The earth has a limited capacity to care for us and is fragile—much more fragile than the industrialists, in their hubris, ever imagined. It is a hard lesson to learn that economic development, to be sustainable, must respect and preserve the life-support systems of the planet.

When the 1992 Earth Summit concluded, then UN Secretary-General Boutros Boutros-Ghali said,

> Over and above the moral contract with God, over and above the social contract concluded with men, we must now conclude an ethical and political contract with nature, with this Earth to which we owe our very existence and which gives us life.

7

The United Nations:
Conscience, Not Enforcer

I have been journeying to the United Nations in New York several times a year for 35 years as a parliamentarian, ambassador, adviser and representative of a non-governmental organization. I have listened to world figures—from Mikhail Gorbachev to Ronald Reagan and Pope John Paul II (twice)—speaking at the great podium in the General Assembly and have even given a couple of speeches there myself. I have known and worked with four secretaries-general: Kurt Waldheim, Javier Perez de Cuellar (who gave me an autographed copy of the UN charter in the organization's six official languages), Boutros Boutros-Ghali and, of course, Kofi Annan. I have been bored in a near-empty General Assembly, as speaker after speaker droned on, and exhilarated at meetings during which you could feel the world getting better due to the handclasps of former enemies. I have attended UN meetings in Geneva, Vienna and Nairobi and travelled to UN health and community centres in the rural regions of Bangladesh, Peru, India and a score of other countries. I chaired the UN's disarmament committee in 1988. The United Nations is part of me. I cannot get it out of my system, and do not desire to. The United Nations is a gift to humanity. In fact, it has lifted up humanity. Lifting up humanity is what global conscience does.

This chapter is not a paean to the UN; I will deal with its faults and mistakes. However, I am not neutral concerning the existence of the UN. In its global strategies for disarmament, economic and social development, environmental protection and the advancement of human rights, the UN has responded to the aching desires for peace and true human security that lie in the hearts of billions of human beings. There is not a person on the planet who is not affected, one way or another, by UN programs.

- **Development.** The Millennium Development Goals reflect the UN's consistent work to raise living standards and human skills. The UN Development Programme operates in 166 countries. UNICEF concentrates on child protection, immunization, girls' education and fighting HIV/AIDS.

- **Democracy.** The UN has provided electoral advice and assistance, including monitoring election results, to more than 90 countries, including Cambodia, Namibia, El Salvador, Eritrea, Mozambique, Nicaragua, South Africa, Kosovo and East Timor.

- **Human rights.** Since the adoption of the Universal Declaration of Human Rights in 1948, the UN has helped enact comprehensive international agreements on political, civil, economic, social and cultural rights. It has focused world attention on cases of torture, disappearance and arbitrary detention, and pressed governments to improve their human rights records.

- **Peacekeeping.** By sending 60 peacekeeping and observer missions to trouble spots around the world, the UN has been able to restore calm sufficiently to allow the negotiating process to go forward, saving millions from becoming casualties of war.

- **Peace-making.** Since 1945, the UN has led negotiations' for more than 170 peace settlements that have ended regional conflicts. These negotiations include those to end the Iran-Iraq war, facilitate the removal of Soviet troops from Afghanistan, and end the civil wars in El Salvador and Guatemala.

- **Environment.** The UN's Global Environment Facility works on global environmental problems such as climate change, ozone layer depletion, toxic waste, loss of forests and species, and air and water pollution. Under a treaty known as the Montreal Protocol, the UN has stimulated governments to phase out chemicals that deplete the ozone layer, sparing millions of people from skin cancer due to exposure to ultraviolet radiation.

- **Nuclear proliferation.** Through the International Atomic Energy Agency, the UN helps to ensure that countries using nuclear technologies are not secretly developing nuclear weapons. The agency safeguards hundreds of nuclear facilities in 70 countries.

- **Culture of peace.** Through the work of UNESCO, the UN has developed the concept of a culture of peace. This is an approach to life that seeks to transform a culture that tends towards war and violence into one in which dialogue, respect and fairness govern social relations.

- **Self-determination.** When the UN was established, a third of the world's population lived in colonies. The UN played a leading role in bringing independence to more than 80 countries. It helped to bring about the downfall of apartheid in South Africa.

- **War criminals.** UN tribunals established for the former Yugoslavia and for Rwanda have convicted war criminals and put them behind bars, and have developed important case law on genocide and human rights. In addition, more than 500 multilateral treaties—on human rights, terrorism, international crime, refugees, disarmament, commodities and the oceans—have been enacted through the UN.

- **Refugees.** More than 50 million refugees fleeing war, famine and persecution have received aid from the UN High Commissioner for Refugees. In 2006, there were 19 million refugees, asylum-seekers and internally displaced persons around the world, mostly women and children, receiving food, shelter, medical aid and education.

- **Women's rights.** The UN Development Fund for Women works to eliminate violence against women, reverse the spread of HIV/AIDS and increase women's access to work and their rights to land. Special UN conferences on the rights of women have led to legislation in many countries to protect women's rights.

- **Child mortality.** In 1960, nearly one in five children in the developing countries died before the age of five. Through oral rehydration therapy, water, sanitation and other health and nutrition measures undertaken by UN agencies, child mortality rates in the developing countries had dropped to less than one in 12 in 2002.

- **Business interests.** The UN has helped businesses by negotiating universally accepted technical standards in statistics, trade law, customs procedures, intellectual property, aviation, shipping and telecommunications. The UN Industrial Development Organization promotes investment, technology transfer and sustainable industrial development in many countries.

- **Clearing landmines.** The UN is leading an international effort to clear landmines in 30 countries, including Afghanistan, Angola, Bosnia and Herzegovina, Mozambique and the Sudan. These mines still kill and maim thousands of innocent people every year.

- **Combatting terrorism.** The UN has put in place the legal framework to combat international terrorism. Thirteen global legal instruments have been negotiated under UN auspices, including treaties against hostage-taking, aircraft hijacking, terrorist bombings, terrorism financing and nuclear terrorism. A new comprehensive convention against terrorism is planned.

- **Indigenous people.** The Permanent Forum on Indigenous Issues has exposed injustices against the 370 million indigenous people who live in 70 countries and are among the most disadvantaged and vulnerable groups of people in the world, and works to improve their economic and social conditions.

Where Failure Lies

While not unknown, the ongoing accomplishments of the United Nations, such as those listed above, are not the stuff of the daily news. What are trumpeted, the nature of the news business being what it is, are the mistakes and failures. The most famous of these were the UN's inability to stop the genocides that took place in Cambodia, Rwanda and Bosnia. Immense killings did take place and the UN did not stop them. There have been scandals and weakness in UN management, showing failures of discipline, financial control and accountability on the part of staff and management. And the continuing saga of UN reform, particularly of the composition of the Security Council, plays out like a never-ending soap opera. The UN is by no means perfect.

But the real value of the UN becomes clear when its accomplishments are weighed against its failures, when the monies expended for peace are weighed against the monies expended for war, when the UN-led building of international law is weighed against any piece of national legislation anywhere. Only those who dislike or fear a supranational organization reaching out to embrace all peoples of all cultures beyond the narrow confines of nationalism remain blind or resistant to the most remarkable means of bringing humanity together that has ever existed.

United Nations Peacekeeping
www.un.org/Depts/dpko/dpko

"... To alleviate human suffering, and create conditions and build institutions for self-sustaining peace." This is the aim pursued by the United Nations Department of Peacekeeping Operations (DPKO). With 70,000 uniformed personnel active in 2006 on projects and more than one million citizens of 130 countries having served in the past, DPKO is the most widely deployed on-the-ground project in history. Its 60 missions since its inception in 1948 have brought people together from all corners of the world.

In 1988, the Nobel Peace Prize was awarded to the United Nations Peacekeeping Forces, which "represent the manifest will of the community of nations" and have "made a decisive contribution" to the resolution of conflict around the world. Additionally, the DPKO has provided an important opportunity for citizens of emerging nations to make positive contributions towards the alleviation of human suffering and the cultivation of self-sustaining peace. The top 10 contributing nations are Bangladesh (10,172 peacekeepers), Pakistan (9,630), India (8,996), Jordan, Nepal, Ethiopia, Uruguay, Ghana, Nigeria and South Africa. DPKO has successfully contributed to self-sustaining peace in countries such as El Salvador and Mozambique.

The UN has no taxation power. It cannot legislate into existence its strategies to counter economic and social inequity. The most it can do to stop war is to enforce a Security Council resolution that itself is subject to veto by any one of the five permanent members. The quarrels among the P5, as they are known, are legendary and have blocked the Council from taking firm action on occasions too numerous to count. The United Nations charter begins with the enchanting, even mesmerizing, words, "We the peoples of the United Nations determined to save succeeding generations from the scourge of war ... ."This gives the impression that the palpable public will for peace will prevail. But no such thing happens. The UN is the place where governments assemble to do diplomatic jousting, jealous of their own powers, in the case of the major players, and fearful of being trampled on, in the case of the small states.

When General Roméo Dallaire warned UN headquarters of the coming slaughter in Rwanda and pleaded for help, it was not "the UN" that failed; rather, it was the obstinacy, the carelessness and the refusal of the major governments to act in the crisis that prevented the UN from stopping the killings. It is not the UN that is responsible for the pileup of armaments in the world that, in the case of small arms, leads directly to wars and human suffering and, in the case of nuclear weapons, threatens the existence of the planet; it is the governments that refuse to agree on either a treaty to block the arms trade or a nuclear weapons convention to shut off forever the production of nuclear weapons. It is certainly not the UN that is responsible for the plight of the poor, hungry and homeless of the world but the governments of the wealthy countries that refuse to back up their protestations of concern for the dispossessed with sufficient cold, hard cash. In all these matters, the UN is a conscience, not an enforcer.

It is galling to observe the UN accused of "not doing enough" when the major powers prevent it from exerting any power to, for example, assemble a permanent, armed peacekeeping force ready to be deployed into a troubled region. The UN's Millennium Development Goals could easily be reached with just a fraction of the money governments spend on arms. In fact, the total annual spending for all UN activities, which includes administration, programs and peacekeeping, is around $10 billion, a tiny fraction of the $1.1 trillion governments spend each year on their militaries. This outlandish discrepancy is not pointed out to the taxpaying public, which might well revolt if it ever fully understood how the conditions for peace could be built for far less than it is now paying to prepare and fight wars, as I noted in chapter 5. Instead, it is the shortcomings of the UN that are constantly brought to public attention, which undermines public confidence in the very instrument dedicated to the evolution of global society along ethical lines.

When there is scandal in the UN, the naysayers come out in force. An "oil for food" program in Iraq before the 2003 war became corrupted. An independent investigation led by former US Federal Reserve Chairman Paul Volker detailed how Saddam Hussein was able to siphon nearly $2 billion from the program. The former head of the program was accused of skimming off $190,000. If this occurred, it was the UN that was defrauded, not the UN doing the defrauding. Still, the UN took the blame. The Volker panel said, "Neither the Security Council nor the Secretariat leadership was clearly in command. That turned out to be a recipe for the dilution of Secretariat authority and evasion of responsibility at all levels."

What government in the world has ever been free from corrupt officials seeking to manipulate the system to their own advantage? This is not to excuse corruption wherever it exists but to make the point that it is less than realistic to expect a worldwide organization composed of thousands of officials from many cultures and operating in six official languages to be a model of administrative perfection. The vast majority of UN staff is talented, highly skilled and devoted to the organization, and some UN workers have paid with their lives for their dedication to the job. But the fiercest critics, who are usually found on the far right of the political spectrum, seize on any scandal or perceived failure to discredit the organization when they do not decry its very existence.

All secretaries-general have been inhibited from speaking out publicly and criticizing the major powers for their shortsighted undermining of the potential of the UN. When Boutros Boutros-Ghali stated publicly that the UN was "indispensable" in the struggle for peace, obviously responding to US Secretary of State Madeleine Albright's earlier contention that the US was "indispensable," he paid the price. Although 14 members of the Security Council voted for his re-election as secretary-general in 1996, the US vetoed it, and Boutros-Ghali was gone. His successor, Kofi Annan, went to great lengths to placate the hostility of such far-right US opponents as former Senator Jesse Helms, and swallowed hard at the Bush administration's unilateralism, which derailed many UN strategies. But when he allowed himself to say that the US war in Iraq was "illegal," he endangered his working relationship with the US. The US administration, which had bypassed the UN in its pursuit of the war, took umbrage. Annan, in the last months of his tenure, had to mute his criticism, despite the unfolding Iraq catastrophe, for the greater good of the organization. Annan had to look to the future, beyond the Bush administration and beyond his own tenure, to a time when the world might suddenly wake up and realize that the surest way to peace is to implement the international law advocated by myriad UN resolutions.

The UN's Crisis of Confidence

In the meantime, in these opening years of the 21st century, when the world is beset by the inflammatory combination of war, poverty, terrorism and climate change, the UN must overcome its own crisis of confidence. The crisis revolves not just around money, in short supply as it is, or enforcement power, stripped by Security Council wrangling as it is, but particularly around credibility. Is the UN, conceived by the victors of World War II, born into a world of 2.4 billion people and joined by 51 founding states, now capable of responding to the needs of 6.5 billion people in a multi-challenged, globalized world of 192 states? Is the UN capable of meeting the challenges of war and peace in the 21st century? Is it stultified in the way it does business? Despite its 60-year record, the UN must prove its credibility in the face of the threats of nuclear proliferation, terrorism and extreme poverty.

Thus, however maddening it is when the Western media and governments upend the truth by claiming that the UN's weakness and not their own hypocrisy is responsible for disorder today, the UN must be reformed. The UN, despite the obstacles it faces, must show that it can work. Even though the essential problem is the attitude of governments and not the international mechanism they have created, the question of UN reform must be addressed. Reform of the UN is a surrogate for the reform of government interaction in the age of globalization. In agreeing on ways to strengthen the UN, governments may find the way to adapt their current selfish policies to the common good.

Security Council Membership

The Secretary-General's High-level Panel on Threats, Challenges and Change devoted a considerable portion of its report to this subject. It called, first of all, for the General Assembly, the principal deliberative body, to restrain if not eliminate its "repetitive, obscure" debates and resolutions and focus on the most compelling issues of the day. But the real problem lies in the makeup of the Security Council, which has primary responsibility for maintaining international peace and security. The five permanent members were given veto rights—indeed, they would not have joined without them—but were also expected to shoulder the extra burden of promoting global security. It continues to be a contradiction of the first order that the P5 are the nations brandishing nuclear weapons. Not only are they delinquent in their obligations under the Non-Proliferation Treaty to engage in comprehensive negotiations to eliminate nuclear weapons, their example has been to rely on nuclear weapons for their own security while admonishing the rest of the world not to join the nuclear club.

World Federation of UN Associations
www.wfuna.org

The UN charter opens with the words "We the peoples of the United Nations ... ." The World Federation of UN Associations takes these words seriously. The federation is a network of hundreds of thousands of people linked together through United Nations Associations in 100 member states of the UN. It ensures that the UN is relevant to the lives of the peoples it exists to serve. This entails campaigning in support of the Millennium Development Goals, human rights, peace and conflict prevention, bridging the digital divide, and sponsoring model UN events. This worldwide network enables people to connect with one another on critical global issues affecting humanity, from peace and human rights to the spread of democracy, equitable development and international justice.

The federation also offers insights into what the UN is and how it works, and is a channel through which people can join to become engaged in the critical global issues affecting the world. The federation maintains partnerships and alliances with several other organizations whose objectives include support for the UN and its development. On the ground, it has played an important role by aiding people in countries where human rights have been violated, such as in Spain under Franco, in some of the formerly Communist states in Eastern Europe, and in the Middle East. It has brought together people of divided countries, such as East and West Germany and Cyprus, and the opponents in conflicts, such as Israel and Egypt in the late 1960s.

This inconsistency, plus the Council's unwillingness to act in the face of genocides or other atrocities when one or more of the permanent members has some interest in not acting, has diminished the Council's credibility. The damage to credibility worsens as the imbalance in permanent membership continues. In effect, now that Russia has for all intents and purposes joined the West in its economic and military policies, four of the five seats are held by Western nations; only China comes from Asia, which contains half the world's population. By what modern standard could the UK and France, whose combined population is one tenth the size of India, each justify their continued hold on a veto-wielding seat while India sits on the sidelines? The entire continents of South America and Africa are unrepresented. The composition of the non-permanent members—10 elected by region for a two-year stint—is supposed to introduce geographical balance. But it is the P5 with their veto power who run, and misuse, the Council.

Looking for ways to broaden the decision-making processes of the Council, the High-level Panel set out two models for enlarging the Council. That the panel could not itself agree on one formulation foreshadowed the governments' later inability to agree on what should be done. The panel proposed Model A, providing for six new permanent seats without veto power and three new two-year non-permanent seats, for a new total of 24 seats. All the regions of the world would be represented. Model B provided for no new permanent seats, but proposed creating eight four-year, renewable seats and increasing the current 10 two-year non-renewable seats by one. Again, the grand total would be 24. The idea behind Model B was to strengthen the non-permanent category by opening the way to the top funding nations and greatest contributors to peacekeeping without allowing any more permanent members.

Neither model tampered with the permanence of the P5 or their veto power, although the panel showed its distaste for the continued special rights of the powerful by noting that the veto is "unsuitable for the institution in an increasingly democratic age ... ." Though it could not eliminate the veto (and took as a given that a veto-wielding state would veto any proposal to eliminate the veto), the panel asked that the veto be limited to matters in which vital interests are genuinely at stake and that a P5 state never use it in cases of genocide and other large-scale human rights abuses.

When he responded to the High-level Panel, Annan fully supported the idea of making the Security Council more broadly representative "and thereby more legitimate in the eyes of the world." But he could go no further than merely recommending that states consider both models. Brute political manoeuvring then took over the halls of the UN. Germany, Japan, India and Brazil, which had formed a consortium to attempt to gain permanent seats, stepped up their lobbying. Nigeria, South Africa and Mexico all pressed a claim. Regional jealousies abounded. In the end, when the leaders met for the UN's 60th anniversary summit, they could not agree. The failure of the major states to rise up to the challenge of reforming Security Council membership to meet the demands of the 21st century is a perfect illustration of their inability or unwillingness to fully respond to the pressures of globalization.

Governments' Rhetoric Versus Action

The United Nations is torn by the vestiges of nationalism that still drive international relations; whether these are the last vestiges remains to be seen. The nation-state system, which has been the determining force in world politics for the past three-and-a-half centuries, is guarded by the major players, yet is surely giving way to the globalized world, in which it is evident that no one state, however powerful, can by itself manage problems that sweep across national boundaries. Co-operation has become essential. Whether co-operation will evolve into a new management system for the world is an open question. At the moment, the world leaders allow themselves to be forward-minded in their rhetoric but resist strong action to implement the global strategies they have already identified. One would have difficulty faulting this sentence in the 60th anniversary summit document:

> We pledge to enhance the relevance, effectiveness, efficiency, accountability and credibility of the United Nations system. This is our shared responsibility and interest.

It is as if the leaders see the benefits of a UN that can steer the world through the quagmire of security and resource problems but, in the end, do not want a UN that rivals their own power. They want a UN secretary-general who is more secretary than general. They insist on management reforms of the system, which are all well and good, but do not speak to the real reform needed: making the UN a universal instrument with the power to implement strategies of disarmament, sustainable development and human rights advancement.

Nonetheless, the leaders are by no means impervious to new demands. In addition to formalizing the concept of the responsibility to protect, which I discussed in chapter 3, the 60th anniversary summit document announced the creation of a peace-building commission to fill a need in the UN system for a mechanism to help countries in the transition from war to peace. It will assemble the resources for reconstruction and institution-building efforts. The leaders also mandated the creation of a human rights council to replace the UN Human Rights Commission, which was widely perceived as being plagued by inefficiency and hypocrisy. The new body must do more than co-ordinate human rights work within the UN system; it must restore the UN's credibility in the human rights field, by exposing the racial and religious hatreds that incite violence.

Annan had criticized the old system for allowing states to seek membership in the commission not to strengthen human rights but to protect themselves against criticism or criticize others. Trust among states is low. Annan's successor as secretary-general, Ban Ki-Moon of South Korea, who took office on January 1, 2007, called for more intensive dialogue among states "to cut through the fog of mistrust." In his acceptance speech, the new secretary-general said, "If we choose wisely, and work together transparently, flexibly and honestly, progress in a few areas will lead to progress in many more."

The Potency of Civil Society

Annan, a wise and patient man well deserving of the Nobel Peace Prize he won in 2000, sensed that he had an ally in his quest to lift up UN work. At least three times in his formal response to the High-level Panel, he urged the UN to be open not just to states but also to civil society, "which at both the national and international levels plays an increasingly important role in world affairs." Civil society can mobilize broad-based movements and create grassroots pressure "to hold leaders accountable for their commitments." Since the goals of the UN can be achieved only when civil society and governments are fully engaged, the General Assembly should "establish mechanisms enabling it to engage fully and systematically with civil society."

In 2000, Annan convened a five-day forum to allow representatives of civil society to provide input into the millennium governmental summit. He called the gathering "the NGO Revolution" because it went far beyond protesting against the dark side of globalization; he said civil society could become "the new superpower" in building worldwide campaigns to strengthen multilateral norms and develop legal regimes. Also, Annan created the Civil Society Panel to widen the entry points for civil society to the UN.

On some days, the basement halls of the UN building are teeming with activists trying to exert their influence on intergovernmental processes. But much of this activity is on an ad hoc basis.

The very potency of civil society—whether working within or outside the political system—has already produced a backlash within governments. Some states in Africa, Asia and Latin America find the prodding and exposure of human rights violations by non-governmental organizations annoying. Some powerful European, North American and East Asian states resent non-governmental organization pressure for economic justice, disarmament and global democracy. In the disarmament field, the major states severely limit the access of these organizations, which in many instances know considerably more about the details of disarmament discussions than do the delegates. The Civil Society Panel pointed to this concern: "Governments do not always welcome sharing what has traditionally been their preserve. Many increasingly challenge the numbers and motives of civil society organizations in the United Nations—questioning their representivity, legitimacy, integrity or accountability."

Nonetheless, the role of civil society in the UN is growing and will be helped by this statement in the 60th anniversary summit document:

> We welcome the positive contributions of the private sector and civil society, including non-governmental organizations, in the promotion and implementation of development and human rights programmes and stress the importance of their continued engagement with Governments, the United Nations and other international organizations in these key areas.

It is not inconceivable that some day, though doubtless far off in the future, a directly elected "people's assembly" will be created at the UN. This would indeed be the fulfillment of the opening words of the UN charter. Currently,

attention is focused on strengthening the role of parliamentarians at the UN. The Inter-Parliamentary Union (IPU), an
international organization of 144 parliaments of sovereign
states founded in 1889, has been granted observer status at
the UN. Through annual meetings of parliamentarians at the
UN and at other gatherings, dealing with the full range of
human security issues, the IPU is positioning itself to play
the role of a parliamentary assembly at the UN. It took years
of lobbying and the direct intervention of Secretary-General
Annan to get this far.

The reform of the UN encompasses many things: the
internal issues revolving around more equitable representation, greater efficiency in management, and a strengthening
of the voices of civil society and parliamentarians to more
fully reflect the conscience of the millions who want a life
of human dignity for all; and the external issues shaping
governments' attitudes towards power and protectionism.
Action is taking place on both the internal and external issues, but it is resisted, for the most part, by those who profit
from the status quo, are blind to the unsustainability of a
world of discord, or are ideologically opposed to even the
thought of a world organization with any teeth.

In such turbulent weather does the United Nations
operate, with storms all around it and a few leaks in its
hull. The UN must retain the support of the major states,
especially the United States, because to lose the active involvement of the powerful would lead the UN to the same
fate as its predecessor, the League of Nations, whose credibility was so diminished by major states ignoring it that
it could not prevent the onslaught of World War II. Each
secretary-general has had to steer the ship with great care
to avoid the perilous shoals of excessive nationalism that
could sink it. But the longer the UN endures, the greater
will be its capacity to achieve strength of its own to meet
global challenges that all governments will come to realize
they themselves cannot handle.

Abolition 2000

www.abolition2000.org

In April 1995, the Non-Proliferation Treaty, then 25 years old, was reviewed at the UN to evaluate whether it should be extended indefinitely. Many activists were disappointed that during the review process nuclear abolition was not the main focus. Non-governmental organizations from many countries decided to react by founding Abolition 2000, an international network of organizations working to push governments to sign a treaty to eliminate nuclear weapons over a fixed timeline. The group's 11-point program centred on calling for negotiations to eliminate nuclear weapons. Since then, more than 2,000 groups in 90 nations have joined and are now working to achieve Abolition 2000's original goal of eliminating nuclear weapons.

The Abolition 2000 Network meets every year and maintains ongoing communication with organizations through the Internet, conferences, teleconferencing and periodic mailings. It also works with the Mayors for Peace program, which brings mayors from around the world together in support of concluding negotiations for nuclear disarmament. Abolition 2000 is open to all those in civil society who want to contribute to the abolition of nuclear weapons.

A Force for Social Justice

In what might be termed its middle years (the UN is far from elderly), the organization's greatest contribution is to point the way to new dimensions of international justice and social justice. Although the term *social justice* is not usually found in UN documents, much of the UN's activity is directed at repairing the injustices of poverty and oppression. Extreme poverty and the suffering it entails affect a large part of humanity; discrimination, poor health, vulnerability, insecurity and a lack of personal and professional development opportunities are among the many challenges the poor face. The Millennium Development Goals are an expression of social justice.

The framework of moral values that underpins social justice varies across cultures and over time, but through the centuries prophets and philosophers have repeatedly attempted to identify common ground that would allow all human beings to agree on definitions of right and wrong. What was originally a spiritual concept has entered daily life. The United Nations is an outgrowth and an expression of this quest for the universal, of this purposeful search for a common humanity. The UN labours to establish social justice and international justice as key organizing principles of human society, and its potential in facilitating this process should not be underestimated.

For the UN, international equality is both a guiding principle and a central objective. That is why the charter speaks of "social progress and better standards of life in larger freedom." The presumption is that international co-operation is a moral imperative, necessary for the reduction of inequalities between states. The ideologies of market forces and peace through war sweep aside this quest for the common good. Thus the UN is set back by those who display contempt for international law and are convinced that violence and war are legitimate and effective ways to pursue national interests. The "hard" development of an efficient and dynamic world economy holds sway over the "soft" humanitarian values of a participatory world community.

The credibility of the United Nations revolves around this very point. Were the UN to be met with approval by the military-industrial complex, one could be sure that the founding values of the organization had been jettisoned. Conversely, to the extent that it stands up for the values of equity and fairness, the UN is charged by its opponents as having no credibility. The UN must cut across the cultural values of greed that have produced the wars and suffering of the past century while retaining the support of the powerful who are still in a position to put it out of business.

The UN has, fortunately, been able to elaborate a lengthy list of civil, political, economic and social rights of people. That has been no small achievement. At the moment—one might define this moment as the last gasp of militarism in a global community closing in on peace—it does not seem possible to codify a "third generation" of human rights, focusing on the collective rights of people and including the rights to peace, development and a healthy environment. There are global forces promoting selfishness, greed and the raw exercise of power that do not want private economic and financial forces subjected to international laws and certainly do not want global taxes to support global social programs. But there is an opposite force, composed of many like-minded governments and civil society, promoting the global values of tolerance, diversity and pluralism along with fair trade policies.

While the two forces appear to be at a standoff, this is quite an incomplete way of weighing their relative strengths. The powerful maintain their dominance; this is exactly what they have done through the centuries, which is the point to be noted. The opposing forces calling for equity through the implementation of the UN agenda for peace and human security are, historically speaking, new on the scene. The modern understanding of the phenomenon of globalization is still being formulated. But already great numbers of civil society, for the first time in history, are assembling to pressure the powerful to adopt equitable policies. The UN is not their only instrument to move world opinion, but it is the only instrument in which the governments of the world are participating to form an agenda acceptable to all. It is not a standoff. The movement forward of UN values is occurring despite the resistance of the recalcitrant.

In its first 60 years, the UN has provided the world with a place for every country to assemble and sort out global problems. It has early-warning and assessment mechanisms to deal with threats to security and impose peacemaking. It has created institutions to avert financial crises and bring development programs to hundreds of millions of people. It has established an array of bodies to respond to the needs of the most vulnerable and promote human rights for all. It has set up an international monitoring regime to protect the global environment. The opponents of the UN or those who have lost faith in it should consider this list of accomplishments. The UN, argues the distinguished historian and author Paul Kennedy, belongs to the governments of the world and, much more distantly, to its peoples. "The human race created it, and the human race has inherited it. Parts of it have failed miserably, others have performed wonderfully, just like human beings. But to dismiss the UN's record, as do some contemporary critics, is unfair. Actually, it is absurd."

The United Nations is the world's most potent and hopeful expression of global conscience.

III

New Challenges

8

The Global Conscience
of Religion

Does religion have a global conscience?

That seems a strange question to ask, even a bit humorous or perhaps taunting, considering that religion is supposed to be all about uplifting the human being in accordance with God's will. The reason the question is so pertinent is that religion today has been hijacked by extremists who seek to justify violence in the name of God. The radicalization of religion and those who use religion to promote their own political agenda obscures the commitment to justice and peace that lies at the heart of all faith traditions. It is time for moderates to stand up and reclaim the real beauty and untapped potential for peace in every religion.

The answer to the question of religion having a global conscience is a firm yes. It is precisely because religious communities are the largest and best-organized civil institutions in the world, claiming the allegiance of billions of believers, that they are uniquely equipped to meet modern challenges: resolve conflicts, care for the sick and needy, and promote peaceful coexistence among all peoples.

But confusion about the proper role of religion abounds. Animosities and divisions persist. In the case of the two largest faiths, Christianity and Islam, which together embrace more than half of humanity, the gulf appears to be widening.

The terrorism of 9/11 plunged the world into a renewed cycle of violence just at the moment that the 21st century opened with the hint that a culture of peace might replace the culture of war. Killings mounted. Islam was demonized in the West. Western secularism was vilified by Islamic fundamentalists. "Violence in the name of God" became a perverse slogan of the new age, which showed so tragically how ineffective religion has been at curbing the forces of war. Instead of rising up to cry out with one voice to proclaim peace through our common humanity and the rule of law, religious leaders seem to have been overcome with trying to find the identity for their own religions. A debate has broken out about how people of faith should influence politics. One would have hoped that the debate would be about how to implement the common values of love, compassion and justice. But instead, the debate is over coercion and the pugnacious claim that "God is on our side." Instead of uniting in this moment, which combines both danger and promise for all humanity, religion has become a divisive force.

In his book *Our Endangered Values*, former US President Jimmy Carter warns against blurring the lines between politics and rigid religious fundamentalism.

> During the last two decades, Christian fundamentalists have increasingly and openly challenged and rejected Jesus' admonition to "render to Caesar the things that are Caesar's and to God the things that are God's." Most Americans have considered it proper for private citizens to influence public policy, but not for a religious group to attempt to control the processes of a democratic government or for public officials to interfere in religious affairs or use laws or tax revenues to favor certain religious institutions.

The Christian Right plays a significant role in many elections in Western countries, particularly the United States. This group is defined largely as evangelical with a strong view of biblical authority, opposition to secular and non-Christian influence, and the conviction that believers should separate themselves from the non-Christian world. Their social values revolve around opposition to abortion and gay marriage. They are hostile to the idea of a world based on secular morality and on global institutions such as the United Nations. Their role in getting George W. Bush elected to the US presidency in 2000 and 2004 has been well charted.

The power of the Christian Right to elect their own should not be overdrawn, as the 2006 congressional elections in the US showed. In these elections, there was a return to practical political judgments as to which party or individual candidate could best effect a solution to the apparently intractable problem of the war in Iraq. Nonetheless, the ardour of the Christian Right in affirming its superior understanding of "real" Christianity and opposing ecumenical overtures to build working coalitions with people of other faiths and secular society as a whole continues to weaken the leadership of virtually all the Christian churches.

Similarly, Islam has allowed itself to be seen as weak in the face of the demand by extremists to establish Islamic states throughout the Middle East. Islamic extremists see violence as their tool, especially to express their rage against foreign domination, as in Iraq, but also against the larger economic domination of the West, which produces, not least in the Muslim world, feelings of humiliation. By far the great majority of Muslim leaders condemned the terrorist attacks of 9/11, but it cannot be denied that some Muslim fundamentalists saw just desserts in the collapse of the World Trade Center.

It will take more than a few harmonious interfaith dialogues between Christians, Muslims and Jews to overcome the real source of religious divisions in the world today. Those divisions lie in the attitude of superiority and exclusiveness in which the differences of "the other" are highlighted rather than the commonalities of all, irrespective of race or religion. In a world that is moving, however haltingly, towards the values of a universal civilization, the individualistic autonomy of religions holds back the blossoming of what could be their greatest achievement: that all may be one under God.

The best of religion, of course, espouses this, but self-protection in the face of raging storms allows the Christian Right and the Islamic extremists, to use but two examples, to typify the public face of religion today. The Christian Right would, no doubt, object to being placed in the same sentence as Islamic extremists. But both have distorted, in their own ways, the themes of social justice that mark both Christianity and Islam.

The Christian Right never speaks of the economic violence the "Christian" West has perpetrated against much of the developing world and that has aggrandized three quarters of the wealth of the world. Muslim terrorist groups will continue to recruit successfully as long as a large number of Muslims feel that they are being unfairly targeted and that justice has ceased to matter in world affairs. The deaths of Iraqi people and Afghani people and of children throughout the developing countries, who die every day of starvation, are but statistics, yet every soldier who returns to the West in a coffin is honoured.

The Christian Right and Islamic extremists constantly assign blame for the wrongs of the world to "the other." Hatred and fear become paralyzing instruments in both societies. Extremists, the most radical of whom become terrorists, exploit the persistent economic and social inequities.

To repeat: it is not religion that causes violence in all its forms, but the perpetuation of economic and social injustices that religious extremists exploit. The problem is not in the Bible, the Koran or the Torah but in how extremists seek to justify their political violence by misrepresenting the sacred texts. All religions teach the golden rule: do unto others what you would have done unto you. Yet the Bible, the Koran and the Torah all contain some texts that, taken in isolation, appear to justify violence.

A United Condemnation of Extremism

So serious is the distortion of religion in the carnage-filled aftermath of 9/11 that Christian, Muslim, Jewish, Buddhist, Hindu and Shinto religious leaders in 49 countries held a summit in Moscow in July 2006, on the eve of the G8 meeting of political leaders. The religious leaders condemned terrorism and extremism in any form, as well as attempts to justify them by religion.

> Using religion as a means for rousing hatred or an excuse for crimes against individuals, morality and humanity present a major challenge today. ... We call for an end to any insult to religious feelings and the defilement of texts, symbols, names or places held sacred by believers. Those who abuse sacred things should know that it wounds the hearts and stirs up strife among the people.

Pope Benedict XVI sent five cardinals to the meeting, one of whom, Cardinal Walter Kasper, president of the Pontifical Council for Promoting Christian Unity, enlarged on the theme of misrepresentation of religion.

> We must categorically reject the exploitation, abuse and mis-use of religion, especially when it is used as a pretext for hate, oppression and terrorism. God is a name of peace and cannot be used as an argument for killing innocent people.

The Pope later got into trouble with Muslims for quoting, in an academic lecture, a 14th-century emperor who said Islam was a religion of violence. Pope Benedict later expressed sorrow that he had been misinterpreted, and 38 Muslim leaders publicly accepted this. The Pope later went to Turkey, a predominantly Muslim country, where he was cordially received. The lecture incident, like the public reaction to Danish cartoons lampooning Islam, shows the precarious sensitivity today in Christian-Muslim relations. But such incidents pale by comparison to the outright wars that took place between Christians and Muslims during the time of the Crusades. The relationship between the two religions has actually advanced to such a degree that the Second Vatican Council document *Nostra Aetate* (Declaration on the Relation of the Church to Non-Christian Religions) said the church "esteems" Muslims and praises Islam for its spiritual values. Not much public attention is paid the reconciliatory aspects of the Muslim-Christian relationship, while the media plays up any missteps or irritations. That is why the World Conference of Religions for Peace, meeting in Kyoto in 2006, insisted:

> Religious communities need to express their opposition whenever religion and its sacred principles are distorted in the service of violence.

Participants at a conference in Edmonton in October 2006, "Building World Peace: The Role of Religions and Human Rights," came to the same conclusion: religions must affirm that violence can never be justified in the name of God, and the moderate majority within each religion must assume greater responsibility for becoming the public face of each religious tradition.

These new efforts to have religions reach out not just to one another but also to secular society flow from the emergence of the global conscience of religion. Though distortions on the one hand and timidity on the other still prevail, courageous efforts are under way to let the best, most compassionate values of religion shine in the public square.

The United Nations Conference on Inter-faith Cooperation for Peace was held in June 2005 and led to the forming of a tripartite forum of representatives of member states, UN agencies and non-governmental organizations. The 2005 conference was repeated in 2006, with the Philippines leading a core group of 15 states interested in promoting interfaith dialogue among civilizations, cultures and religions to reinforce tolerance and respect for diversity. President Abdoulaye Wade of Senegal set out the basic issues:

> On what basis does one kill in the name of God? On what basis would one pit Muslims against Christians? How did human societies arrive at confrontation when the real message of religions has always been that of a vehicle for reconciliation and harmony?

The Torah, the Bible and the Koran all teach the uniqueness of God, he said. "They prescribe good and prohibit wrong. They exhort spiritual elevation, preach moderation, forgiveness, charity and love of fellow man." The members of the Inter-Faith Forum, as this smaller group of advocates is known, do not plunge into the theological issues that emerge from historical interpretations of texts. Rather, they dwell on practical measures to bring the abundant rhetoric on interfaith dialogue down to earth, elaborating concrete and sustained activities to promote a culture of peace through better and more respectful dialogue among religions and cultures at the local, national, regional and international levels. The forum is about more than freedom of religion, though it is about that, too; rather, it is about strengthening ways to eliminate all forms of religious intolerance. The forum has targeted co-ordinated actions to prohibit the dissemination of xenophobic and racist materials targeting any religious or ethnic communities.

Inter-Faith Action for Peace in Africa
www.africa-faithforpeace.org

Inter-Faith Action for Peace in Africa (IFAPA) is a peace group comprised of believers in the traditional African religions, Baha'i, Buddhism, Christianity, Hinduism, Islam and Judaism. Created at a historic meeting in October 2002, IFAPA is committed to embracing the gift of peace and to promoting genuine interfaith dialogue and co-operation for peace in Africa. This unique organization seeks to acknowledge that despite the fact that Africa has long been a continent of conflict and violence, faith may be a source of inspiration and a limitless toolset for improving the human condition.

Focusing on the idea that Africa can also be seen as a continent of hope, courage and determination, IFAPA emphasizes the successful fight against apartheid in South Africa, which shows that Africans can turn their continent around for the better. Based on the above principles, IFAPA serves as a communicating mechanism to develop and provide programs on peace, violence reduction, conflict resolution and religious freedom through all of the faith traditions in Africa.

Common Social Justice Values

This pioneering interfaith work at the UN puts a focus on an overarching fact of the modern world: we live in a multi-religious, multicultural and pluralistic world in which all of us, regardless of our conviction, must unite to fight endemic hatred, misrepresentation, misunderstanding and ignorance. Alberto G. Romulo, secretary of foreign affairs for the Philippines, goes further and says that religious collaboration can end civil conflicts, as has occurred in Sierra Leone and Liberia. In these two states, conflict was overcome through the concerted efforts of religious leaders and civil society movements.

So far, it is mostly Asian and Middle Eastern states taking part in the Inter-Faith Forum at the UN. The Western states are notably absent, the rigid separation of church and state doubtless at the forefront of bureaucratic thinking, or an unspoken assumption, as previously noted, of the "superiority" of the West. Interfaith dialogue is not about God invading Caesar's domain; rather, it is about letting light shine on the common values of humanity that have been encapsulated in the Universal Declaration of Human Rights. It is about the humanization of public policy.

Unfortunately, it is not just government officials who are afraid of integrated thinking; there are many religious leaders who are convinced that the sole purpose of religion is to be a vehicle between humankind and God. Such thinking either ignores or greatly diminishes the social responsibilities that flow from the command to love our neighbours as ourselves. The excessive introspection of religionists leads to religious myopia and quarrels. But in the discord of the 21st century, it is already clear that there must be peace among religions if there is to be peace among nations. And there cannot be peace among religions without a genuine, respectful dialogue among religions and between religions and secular society.

A primary place for religions to come together is around their common consideration of social justice issues. This is the very point religious leaders made at their summit in Moscow in 2006: they appealed to governments, religious communities and the peoples of the world to work together to face the problems of poverty, hunger and social vulnerability. They named the problems of infectious disease epidemics (particularly AIDS), drug addiction and the proliferation of weapons of mass destruction as ones to start with.

> No country, regardless of wealth and power, can cope with these threats on its own. We are all inter-connected and share a common destiny. This requires

concerted and united action by all member states of
the international community.

The 2006 World Religions for Peace Conference in
Kyoto took the same approach of seeking practical grounds
for inter-religious co-operation. "War, poverty, disease, and
the destruction of the environment have direct or indirect
impacts on all of us." Religious communities are called on
not only to reject war and foreign occupation, sectarian
violence, weapons proliferation and human rights abuse,
but also to identify and confront the root causes of injustice,
economic inequalities, governance failures, development
obstacles, social exclusions and environmental abuses. "The
efforts of individual religious communities are made vastly
more effective through multi-religious cooperation."

The theme of common religious work for social justice
is repeated in countless religious documents. The World
Council of Churches has been espousing social justice
themes for decades. The Parliament of the World's Religions
calls for a "global ethic" built on the set of core values found
in the teachings of all major religions. This ethic would embrace a culture of non-violence and respect for life, a culture
of solidarity and a just economic order, a culture of tolerance
and truthfulness, and a culture of equal rights and partnership between men and women. In many places, religious
networks are advancing these themes with local projects.
In Canada, the Religious Society of Friends (Quakers)
has called on the government to change its policy and
funding priorities to increase support for the Millennium
Development Goals and "make poverty history," and to end
financial support to industries that produce the instruments
of war.

Faithful Security

www.faithfulsecurity.org

Faithful Security, a group of citizens participating in the National Religious Partnership on the Nuclear Weapons Danger, is dedicated to bringing together religious groups on a local level to break faith with nuclear weapons once and for all. The goal of Faithful Security is to work towards the permanent elimination of nuclear weapons by empowering religious communities to take action on a local level. This ambitious and pluralistic effort includes people from a wide range of faith traditions, including Jews, Protestants, Shintos, Catholics, Muslims, Hindus, Sikhs, Buddhists and others who believe that all human life is sacred. Their toolkit is intended to provide citizens with the resources they need to learn about the danger of nuclear weapons and take action to build a safer world for all their brothers and sisters.

Faithful Security also works with students to educate them about nuclear weapons. Additionally, the group monitors legislation on non-proliferation and new nuclear weapons and maintain a speakers' bureau so that people interested in nuclear weapons issues may have easier access to the experts.

Many people of faith throughout the world want religions to be the solid foundation for peace and dialogue among civilizations, and yet "dialogue among civilizations" needs to be more than a slogan. Religions need to work together to build a world order that combines democracy and respect for morality, legal and political systems, and national and religious traditions. Through education and social action, people can be inspired to support ethical values for sustainable development of the planet.

A concentration on universal social justice themes has marked the teaching of the Catholic church; I want to explore this to show the strong base of social teaching it could bring to a new universal dialogue.

A Thunderous Message

"This poor South will judge the rich North."

Perhaps no other sentence in the panoply of Catholic teaching on poverty, and who is responsible for poverty, so sharply arouses the global conscience. Pope John Paul II uttered—thundered would be a better description—the sentence at a mass I attended in a huge field at the Canadian Forces base at Namao, near Edmonton, on September 17, 1984. The Pope was then touring Canada in the sixth year of his extraordinarily long pontificate. In those days, his stance was firm, his voice resonant, and it was clear by his tone during his homily that the Pope had an exceptionally important message.

He spoke first of the Second Vatican Council's teaching that Christian ethics has a social dimension. The human person lives in a community, sharing with all hunger and thirst, sickness and misery. The "least of the brethren" cannot be isolated from the universal. Then he applied this theme to the widening gap between the wealthy North and the increasingly poorer South. "Yes, the South—becoming always poorer, and the North—becoming always richer." He excoriated the wealthy nations for piling up weapons and threatening each other so as, in the strange logic of the Cold War, not to destroy each other. One could feel the irony in the Pope's words. And then he came to the passage that captured the attention of the crowd:

In the light of Christ's words, this poor South will judge the rich North. And the poor people and poor nations—poor in different ways, not only lacking food, but also deprived of freedom and other human rights—will judge those people who take these goods away from them, amassing to themselves the imperialistic monopoly of economic and political supremacy at the expense of others.

The words seemed to hang over the throng. There was no clapping or cheering. The exuberant crowd had gone still. Everyone knew that the truth had been spoken. The speech was, of course, widely reported. Some observers, following closely the Pope's messages at every stop of the Canadian tour, considered this the high moment. It was impossible not to know exactly where the Pope stood with respect to the gathering crises across the global arena.

The Cold War was at its peak. New tactical nuclear weapons had just been deployed in six European countries. The superpowers of the day, the US and the Soviet Union, were refusing to negotiate. Fifty-seven nuclear weapons tests took place that year. Huge amounts of money were being spent on arms, while the plight of the poorest countries, discriminated against by financial and trading regulations controlled by the North, went unattended. The UN had tried to define the requirements for a new economic order to right the imbalances, but global economic negotiations never got off the ground. The governments of the North, though they apportioned small amounts of aid, simply did not care enough about the incredible suffering of the millions and millions of poor people caught up in the paralysis of the international systems. Pope John Paul saw all this with great clarity. His searing message was a response to the massive social injustices.

Council Message Addressed to All

There is no doubt that the Pope's remarks acted as a catalyst for many, inside and outside the Catholic church. Many caring people heard this message and responded in their own ways, by making donations, joining non-governmental organizations dedicated to development, and even going to developing countries themselves.

John Paul's social teaching had strong roots in the church, particularly in the Second Vatican Council (1962–1965). The Council was called by Pope John XXIII, who issued an encyclical, *Pacem in Terris* (Peace on Earth), that caught world attention for its call to all people of good will—not just Catholics—to join in raising up civilization. This was, in fact, the first time that a church document was addressed to "all men of good will," who are called to a great task: "to establish with truth, justice, love and freedom new methods of relationships in human society." The encyclical dwelled on the responsibility of the public authority in the world to tackle and solve economic, social, political and cultural problems.

People have "the right to live," Pope John XXIII affirmed. They have "the right to bodily integrity … to food, clothing, shelter, medical care, rest, and social services." People are living in the grip of constant fear of war and violence. "Nuclear weapons must be banned." He said, "True and lasting peace among nations cannot consist of the possession of an equal supply of armaments but only in mutual trust." And "in this age which boasts of its atomic power, it no longer makes sense to maintain that war is a fit instrument with which to repair the violation of justice." The United Nations must "adapt its structure and methods of operation to the magnitude and nobility of its tasks."

With his powerful message addressed to all humanity, Pope John drew a road map for peace. His words foreshadowed the Vatican Council's *Gaudium et Spes* (Constitution on the Church in the Modern World), which elaborated on the joys and hopes, the grief and anxieties that we all have, irrespective of religion, race or culture. The Council here presented in a systematic manner the themes of cultures, economic and social life, marriage and the family, peace and the community of peoples in the light of a Christian anthropological outlook and the church's mission. Society, its structures and development must be oriented towards "the progress of the human person." The church put itself, so to speak, in the modern condition, open to the intellectual climate of 20th-century civilization and the dimensions of human culture opened by advances in the historical, social and psychological sciences. The aim is true dialogue, not a one-sided laying down of dictates on the part of the church. International co-operation is needed for the development of all peoples.

The Council coupled its support for universal human rights with a call for the social order to work for the benefit of the human person.

> There must be made available to all [people] everything necessary for leading a life truly human, such as food, clothing, and shelter; the right to choose a state of life freely and to found a family, the right to education, to employment, to a good reputation, to respect, to appropriate information, to activity in accord with the upright norm of one's own conscience, to protection of privacy and to rightful freedom in matters religious too.

Again, the Council spoke to all in its condemnation of total war.

> Any act of war aimed indiscriminately at the destruction of entire cities or of extensive areas along with their population is a crime against God and [humankind itself]. It merits unequivocal and unhesitating condemnation.

The arms race, the Council added, "is an utterly treacherous trap for humanity, and one which injures the poor to an intolerable degree." All war must be outlawed by universal consent.

Development: The New Name for Peace

Pope Paul VI, who became pontiff during the course of the Council, took up the social justice themes and, in his encyclical *Populorum Progressio* (Development of Peoples), urged the richest countries to take up their sacred duty to help the poorest. "Development is the new name for peace," he said. Development that benefits everyone responds to the demands of justice on a global scale that guarantees world-wide peace and makes it possible to achieve a "complete humanism" guided by spiritual values.

The development of peoples has the church's close attention, particularly the development of those peoples who are striving to escape from hunger, misery, endemic diseases and ignorance, of those who are looking for a wider share in the benefits of civilization and a more active improvement of their human qualities, of those who are aiming purposefully at their complete fulfillment.

Paul VI criticized "the scandal of our glaring inequalities not merely in the enjoyment of possessions but even more in the exercise of power."

> The hungry nations of the world cry out to the peoples blessed with abundance. And the Church, cut to the quick by this cry, ask each and every man to hear his brother's plea and answer it lovingly.

He established the Pontifical Council for Justice and Peace to stimulate the Catholic community to promote progress in needy regions and international social justice. He also started the tradition of observing the first day of the year as the World Day of Peace.

Pope John Paul II maintained this denunciation of the world's spending priorities. In an apostolic letter in 2001, he said,

> How can it be that even today there are still people dying of hunger? Condemned to illiteracy? Lacking

the most basic medical care? Without a roof over their head? The scenario of poverty can extend indefinitely, if in addition to its traditional forms we think of its newer patterns. These latter often affect financially affluent sectors and groups which are nevertheless threatened by despair at the lack of meaning in their lives, by drug addiction, by fear of abandonment in old age or sickness, by marginalization or social discrimination … . And how can we remain indifferent to the prospect of an ecological crisis which is making vast areas of our planet uninhabitable and hostile to humanity? Or by the problems of peace, so often threatened by the spectre of catastrophic wars? Or by contempt for the fundamental human rights of so many people, especially children?

Pax Christi

www.paxchristi.net

Pax Christi was created in France in 1945 to begin reconciling France and Germany at the end of World War II. Now it operates in more than 60 countries and, as a non-governmental organization, has a presence at the United Nations. It actively participates in UNESCO, the UN Commission on Human Rights and the Council of Europe. With principles deriving from the Sermon on the Mount, the focus of the organization is research into solutions to armed conflicts. Pax Christi's efforts are divided among security and armed conflict, economic factors of armed conflict, human rights, the rule of law and armed conflict, conflict transformation, peace building, and youth work and peace education.

For its research, Pax Christi was awarded the Prize for Peace Education from UNESCO in 1983. Pax Christi serves as a member of the International Coalition for the Decade of the Culture of Peace and Nonviolence. It continues to bring faith-based principles to the pursuit of improving human security throughout the world.

Reasons for Humility

This continuum of vigorous defence of the poor and castigation of the rich—particularly over the past four decades, which coincides with the implementation of the Universal Declaration of Human Rights—has been a cry of conscience by the church. Very often it has not been heard or, at least, it has been lost in the next cycle of news headlines. Over the years, far more attention has been paid to whether the "liberals" or "conservatives" are responsible for the dislocation in the post–Vatican II church than to the Council's insistence on public policies to uphold the dignity of the human being. Pope Paul VI is remembered not for *Populorum Progressio* but for his other major encyclical, *Humanae Vitae* (On the Regulation of Birth), which restated the church's proscription of birth control. For all his fame, Pope John Paul II's opposition to a married clergy and the ordination of women caused far more stir in the church than his pleas for social justice. In later years, episcopal preoccupation with sexual abuse by a small but highly publicized minority of priests seemed to drain church energy (and finances) away from concerted efforts to promulgate the social teaching of both the Council and the popes.

All of this is to say that the church has every reason to practise humility in the exposition of its social doctrines. The lavish lifestyle of some bishops (fortunately, a dwindling number), the avoidance of social teaching from the pulpit and even the mixed messages of the popes themselves about their real priorities have all tended to diminish the impact of the conscience-raising core of the social teaching. But the social teaching itself is greater than any teacher. It speaks to the values of humanity and human affairs in their totality. It is, in essence, an appeal to the global conscience.

Of course, the laity has by no means signalled that it welcomes any afflictions in the comfortable pew. Far from being eager to absorb the challenge to Christianity to uplift the world from its morass of war and poverty, church-going Catholics appear to prefer appeals to improve their personal holiness. In the overall context of lassitude in implementing the church's call to social justice, it is remarkable that the teaching has been so consistent, if underappreciated.

In 2005, the Pontifical Council for Justice and Peace published *A Compendium of the Social Doctrine of the Church*, under the direction of Cardinal Renato Martino. The proclamation of Jesus Christ—the Good News of salvation, love, justice and peace—is not readily received in today's world, devastated as it is by wars, poverty and injustices, Martino noted. He appealed for dialogue and co-operation in serving the common good.

The compendium makes the point that humanity is coming to understand ever more clearly that it is linked by one sole destiny that requires joint acceptance of responsibility inspired by an integral and shared humanism. Thus, the church's social teaching proposes "a humanism that is up to the standards of God's plan of love in history, an integral and solidarity humanism capable of creating a new social, economic and political order, founded on the dignity and freedom of every human person, to be brought about in peace, justice and solidarity."

The fullness of this teaching leads to denunciation of injustice and violence that violates human rights, especially those of the poor and the weak. Liberation from everything that oppresses people is sought as a basis for development of the whole person. Greater moral awareness and action are sought to build public policies that reflect justice. In all of this, the awakened conscience is directed outwards towards the good of the whole society.

Speaking Out Without Domination

Moving from the principles of social justice to specific applications continues to challenge church leaders. Their teaching is often, in a secular culture, consigned to the library shelves unless it provokes political leaders. One example of a provocation was the document *Ethical Reflections on the Economic Crisis*, produced in 1983 by the Social Justice Committee of the Canadian Conference of Catholic Bishops. The document directly challenged the policies of the Canadian government, which, at the time, was fighting inflation by raising unemployment levels. The committee's chairman, Bishop Remi De Roo, said the document's purpose was to awaken a national response to a major moral issue: ruthless government polices whereby the "survival of the fittest" triumphed over the needs of the poor and marginalized members of society. The statement's central argument, that the rights of workers are more important than the maximization of profits, was but a local reflection of the universal teaching of the church. But the statement, which of course drew widespread media coverage, also created the impression that the bishops were intruding into the field of Caesar. Had the bishops suddenly become experts on the feasibility and details of macro-economic policies? In this case, the bishops' interventionist stance was further complicated by Vatican II's designation of the laity (not the clergy) as the people to carry the fight for social justice into the political arena. If the bishops got into the arena with solutions to every ongoing problem, would not the public acceptance of their principled positions be compromised?

In short, the sting of public backlash has hurt many bishops when their statements have been criticized for crossing the line between church and state matters. As a result, many bishops are inclined to speak in generalities. On the occasions when they speak out directly, such as opposing the Iraq war or publicly rebuking politicians for pro-abortion positions, they risk dividing the faithful. Thus, they struggle to find ways to speak up for social justice that can be heard and not resented. Since mistakes of one kind or another are inevitable, many bishops are inclined to leave controversial questions to the laity.

A valiant core of lay activists, along with priests and sisters bringing their ministry to the marketplace, have often been the instruments of social teaching: for example, in establishing co-ops. But, generally, the laity has not shown a driving desire to lead the way in putting flesh on the bones of Catholic social teaching. Yet it is evident that the church is called to deal in a more vigorous manner with the problems fracturing humanity today: poverty, drugs, environmental destruction and the excesses of militarism.

The conscience of the church has been clearly awakened to the griefs and sorrows of a struggling humanity. This itself is a tremendous achievement, given the church's long preoccupation with interiority. Its prophecy in discerning the signs of the times—the demand for human rights clashing with the spread of weapons of mass destruction—may still be rebuffed. But the spiritual call to raise all of humanity to live in human dignity in the new age of globalization has clearly been made.

It remains for all people of faith to overcome their introspection and to humbly work for the human rights of all individuals to be integrated into public policies for human security.

9

Alliance, Not Clash, of Civilizations

Culture of peace and initiatives on dialogue among cultures, civilizations and religions

We reaffirm the Declaration and Programme of Action on a Culture of Peace as well as the Global Agenda for Dialogue among Civilizations and its Programme of Action adopted by the General Assembly and the value of different initiatives on dialogue among cultures and civilizations, including the dialogue on interfaith cooperation. We commit ourselves to taking action to promote a culture of peace and dialogue at the local, national, regional and international levels and request the Secretary-General to explore enhancing implementation mechanisms and to follow up on those initiatives. In this regard, we also welcome the Alliance of Civilizations initiative announced by the Secretary-General on 14 July 2005.

—UN 60th anniversary summit document, 2005

It is not likely that many people read the above paragraph, Number 144, tucked away as it is in the document world leaders issued at their summit at the United Nations in 2005. Certainly, the media virtually ignored it. Yet it contains the seeds for a blossoming of humanity never seen before.

The passage refers to the work the UN started in the 1990s to develop the concept of a culture of peace. UNESCO at the time was led by Federico Mayor of Spain, who championed a culture of peace as an approach to life that seeks to transform a culture that tends towards war and violence into one in which dialogue, respect and fairness govern social relations. UNESCO began to flesh out the idea of a culture of peace as a set of ethical and aesthetic values, habits and customs, attitudes towards others and forms of behaviour that stress respect for life and the dignity and human rights of individuals and the rejection of violence.

Mayor's work led to the UN General Assembly adopting, in 1999, the Declaration and Programme of Action on a Culture of Peace. The decade 2001–2010 was designated the International Decade for a Culture of Peace and Non-violence for the Children of the World. Each year would have a different theme, with the UN Year of Dialogue Among Civilizations being the first. Pilot education projects and petitions were developed around the world. UNESCO organized a high-level dialogue, which was incorporated into a book, *Crossing the Divide: Dialogue Among Civilizations*.

Then 9/11 struck. The UN became consumed with the aftermath of terrorism. The bombing of Afghanistan, the war in Iraq and the escalation of conflicts in the Middle East all shoved the idea of a culture of peace into the shadows. Once more, the world spotlight was on war, with all its agonies and suffering. Governments strengthened the resources of militarism to combat terrorism. Despite the futility of war as a means of securing peace, the US and its supporting governments forged ahead. Insurgencies against the American occupation of Iraq produced mayhem, and suddenly mid-east warfare seemed to pit the West against Muslims.

Was the predicted "clash of civilizations" now taking place? A few years earlier, the American scholar Samuel Huntington published *The Clash of Civilizations*, which held as its basic premise that the Muslim world as a monolithic whole is historically and genetically incapable of peace and is intrinsically opposed to a monolithic "Western world." The two are destined to fight. Both Western and Muslim scholars debunked Huntington's theory, but it nonetheless proved an ideological boon for all those who share an interest in worsening hostility between Muslims and the West. By promoting the misguided view that cultures are set on an unavoidable collision course, negotiable disputes are turned into seemingly intractable identity-based conflicts.

The next major terrorist attack occurred in Madrid on March 11, 2004, when trains were bombed, killing 191 people. Again, as in 9/11, the perpetrators were young Muslim men. This provoked among the Spanish memories of the Christian-Muslim wars of the Crusades, 500 years earlier. But rather than reacting provocatively, Spanish President Rodriguez Zapatero proposed in the UN General Assembly that an "alliance of civilizations" project be created as an international response to the terrorist attacks. Zapatero said that Spain had been created and enriched by diverse cultures, and pleaded with the international community to prevent hatred and incomprehension from building a wall between the Western and the Arab and Muslim worlds, leading to a "clash of civilizations." In contrast, the "alliance of civilizations" would reaffirm the increasing interdependence of all societies in the areas of economics, finance, security, culture, environment and health. The central aim of the alliance would be to strengthen diversity so it became a source of enrichment and not a threat.

The Turkish government, with its eye constantly on both Europe and the Islamic world, was also interested in the idea of promoting harmony among cultures and civilizations. Turkish Prime Minister Recep Tayyip Erdogan joined Zapatero in co-sponsoring the alliance initiative. Since Spain and Turkey agreed to be the chief funders, Secretary-General Annan decided to bypass prolonged General

Assembly debate and simply announced the initiative, which would take the form of a High-level Group.

Transparency International
www.transparency.org

Corruption in politics? Enter Transparency International, an international non-governmental organization working to reduce political corruption. Its annual report, the Corruptions Perceptions Index, is a comparative listing of corruption around the world. Headquartered in Berlin, the group has 100 national branches and is likely the leading anti-corruption organization in the world. Its mission is to "create change towards a world free of corruption." Transparency International rejects the notion of "northern superiority" and is committed to exposing corruption in any country. In addition to the Corruption Perceptions Index, it also publishes the annual Global Corruption Report, the Global Corruption Barometer and the Bribe Payers Index. The organization does not pursue investigations or expose individual cases. Instead, it develops tools for fighting corruption and partners with other civil society organizations to implement them. Transparency International focuses on getting the topic of corruption on the world's agenda. Thanks in part to its work, financial institutions such as the World Bank and the International Monetary Fund now see corruption as one of the primary impediments to development and economic reform. This stands in stark contrast to the 1990s, when the topic was seldom discussed. Additionally, Transparency International has performed a valuable role in the development of the UN convention against corruption and the Organization for Economic Co-operation and Development's anti-bribery convention.

Federico Mayor, who had become President of the Culture of Peace Foundation in Spain, and Professor Mehmet Aydin, Minister of State of Turkey and a theologian, were named co-chairs. Other notable members included former President Seyed Mohamed Khatanu of Iran, Nobel laureate Archbishop Desmond Tutu of South Africa, and Karen Armstrong, religious historian.[8] The group's task was to assess new and emerging threats to international peace and security, in particular the political, social and religious forces that foment extremism, and to identify actions to strengthen mutual understanding, respect and shared values among various people. After meeting for a year, the High-level Group released its report. The rest of this chapter deals principally with what the group found.

Globalization Challenging Group Identities

Political and technological developments during the 20th century raised hope for and the possibility of an un-precedented period of harmony among nations and a vast improvement in global well-being. Multilateral co-operation and civil society activism paved the way to a number of positive developments in international relations, including a ban on the use of landmines, the establishment of the International Criminal Court and co-operative work to fight poverty. Despite these achievements, there is a widespread perception that multilateral institutions are failing to im-prove general well-being, putting today's youth at risk. More than half of humanity still leads a life of deprivation. Health and education systems in developing countries remain in-adequate. Destruction of the environment is intensifying. Proliferation of nuclear, biological and chemical weapons escapes effective control.

In all of this, the West is both driving globalization and yet seemingly threatened by some of its trends. Though the major Western nations maintain overwhelming political, economic and military power, they fear porous borders, mounting population flows from poor to rich countries and

---

[8]   See the notes for chapter 9 for the complete list of the members of the High-level Group.

unintegrated immigrant communities. There is a growing perception that developed countries are mainly interested in protecting their own rights. This environment offers fertile ground for the emergence of identity-based politics, which can, in turn, lead to violent tensions among communities.

The inexorable push towards a globalized world has challenged group identities in many parts of the world: the Middle East, Africa, Asia and Latin America. In political systems that offer no channel for grievances to be heard, political and militant groups often emerge, using violence to achieve redress. Perceived as liberation movements by some, they are considered by others as threats to national security systems. At the extreme end of the spectrum, radicals vying for economic or political gain can exploit feelings of humiliation or deprivation to attract recruits for political parties or militant groups formed along religious or ethnic lines.

As we saw in chapter 8, the exploitation of religion by ideologues intent on swaying people to their causes has led to the misguided perception that religion itself is a root cause of intercultural conflict. In some cases, fundamentalist and extremist ideologies have been used to justify acts of violence and even terrorist attacks on civilians. The High-level Group emphasized that none of the world's religions condones or approves the killing of innocents. All promote the ideals of compassion, justice and respect for the dignity of life.

> Recently, a considerable number of acts of violence and terrorism have been committed by radical groups on the fringes of Muslim societies. Because of these actions, Islam is being perceived by some as an inherently violent religion. Assertions to this effect are at best manifestly incorrect and at worst maliciously motivated. They deepen divides and reinforce the dangerous mutual animosity among societies.

The group pointed out that no single group, culture, geographic region or political orientation had a monopoly on extremism and terrorist acts in the 20th century. In fact, secular political motives were responsible for some of the most horrifying reigns of terror in living memory, such as the Holocaust, the Stalinist repressions in the Soviet Union and more recent genocides in Cambodia, the Balkans and Rwanda, all perpetrated by state powers.

However, when communities believe they face discrimination, humiliation and marginalization based on ethnic or religious identity markers, they are likely to assert their identity more aggressively. Collective anger overwhelms moderates' efforts to seek redress. The only durable solution lies in addressing the roots of the resentment and anger that make exclusivist and violent ideologies attractive in the first place. Nowhere have exclusivist ideologies, adversarial perceptions, cultural arrogance and media stereotypes combined more dangerously with conflicts bred of perceived and real injustices than in relations between Western and Muslim societies.

Muslim Countries in Transition

Notwithstanding historical periods of tensions between Christianity, Islam and Judaism, the High-level Group recalled that peaceful coexistence, beneficial trade and reciprocal learning have been the hallmarks of relations between the three major monotheistic religions. During medieval times, Islamic civilization was a major source of innovation, knowledge acquisition and scientific advancement that contributed to the emergence of the Renaissance and Enlightenment in Europe. Similarly, in recent centuries, political, scientific, cultural and technological developments in the West have influenced many aspects of life in Muslim societies and many Muslims have sought to immigrate to Western nations, in part for the political freedoms and economic opportunities.

The rise in modern hostility between Western and Muslim societies lies not in the ancient past but in developments in the last two centuries, starting with European imperialism and the resulting emergence of anticolonial movements. The partition of Palestine by the United Nations in 1947, envisioning the establishment of two states—Palestine and Israel—with a special status for Jerusalem, led to the establishment of the state of Israel in 1948. This began a chain of events that continues to be one of the most tortuous in relations between Western and Muslim societies. Western prosperity built on Middle East oil has proved another source of division. The Taliban seizure of Afghanistan and support of Al Qaeda terrorists led to forceful retaliation after 9/11. The US justified, in part, its invasion of Iraq by a supposed link between Iraq and Al Qaeda. But this link was never established, and Muslim societies perceived unjust aggression by the West.

Both Muslim and Western societies accuse each other of double standards in the application of international law and the protection of human rights. Muslims feel vulnerable to targeted killings, torture, arbitrary detention and renditions. Some Westerners have asserted that Islam is inherently violent, and the rise of Islamophobia exacerbates Muslim fears of the West. Western military operations are widely condemned by Muslims, but sectarian violence between Shias and Sunnis in some Muslim countries and the atrocities committed against civilians in Darfur have not led to widespread condemnation in the Muslim world. These reciprocal perceptions of double standards undermine relations between Muslim and Western societies.

The Muslim countries are themselves in transition, with internal debates between progressive and regressive forces playing out on a range of social and political issues. There appears to be a growing realization among Muslims that authoritarianism and conformity are severe detriments in an increasingly integrated and interdependent world. But moderates have to contend with self-proclaimed religious figures who advocate distorted interpretations of Islamic teachings. Such figures misportray practices such as honour killings, corporal punishment and oppression of women as religious requirements. These practices not only contravene internationally agreed human rights standards but, in the eyes of respected Muslim scholars, have no religious foundation.

Who prevails in these intra-Muslim struggles is central not only to the future of Muslim societies but also to their future relations with the rest of the world. Propagation by Western media and official authorities of oversimplified explanations that either blame Islam as a religion or that falsely pit secularists against religious activists has a detrimental effect. This includes media coverage that gives time and space only to the most extreme of the religious voices in the Muslim world and to the most anti-Muslim ideologues in the West to counter them.

Clearly, distinctions need to be made between, on the one hand, national Muslim movements that resist foreign occupation and, on the other hand, terrorist groups with global ambitions. Resistance groups should be helped to pursue their goals through non-violent participation in political processes. This would counter the appeal of global terrorist groups for whom "clash of civilizations" is a potent slogan to attract a loosely knit network of operatives and supporters. The High-level Group, of course, condemned all violence, regardless of its source or reason.

The group made a number of practical suggestions for ending the prolonged Israeli-Palestinian conflict, the violence in Afghanistan and the war in Iraq. But the long-range value of the report is its suggestions to overcome the mutual fear, suspicion and ignorance across cultures that have spread beyond political leaders into the hearts and minds of populations. The report calls for stronger education, youth, migration and media policies to reduce cross-cultural tensions and build bridges between communities.

Burma Watch International
www.burmawatch.org

Burma Watch International (BWI) was founded in 1989 by Burmese citizens now living in Canada who are concerned about the plight of citizens in their home country. By leveraging freedom of speech and assembly in Canada, BWI seeks to promote public awareness of the social, cultural and economic situation of people in Burma and to provide humanitarian assistance to refugees. As a result, BWI partners with several other non-governmental organizations to host talks, seminars, cultural events and video shows. They also provide regular updates to the public on the situation in Burma.

Now known as Myanmar, a nation of 50 million people, Burma was a territory of Britain and later held by the Japanese. It has been ruled by a military regime since 1962. In 1990, free elections were held, but the military refused to transfer power to the democratically elected government led by Aung San Suu Kyi, who has since been under house arrest. BWI campaigns for the release of this Nobel peace laureate.

Necessary Education Steps

The primary approach to building an alliance of civilizations is education in its various forms, including music, sports, art, drama and film. Such broad perspectives encourage young people to steer away from the kind of exclusivist thinking that holds that one group's interests may be advanced at the expense of others', or that one group's victimization justifies the victimization of others. Civic and peace education offer ways to address issues of identity and foster respect for diversity. It is necessary for nations with increasingly multi-religious and multi-ethnic populations to develop inclusive education about the world and its peoples. The inadequacy of current educational approaches to Muslim-Western relations is reflected in a number of polls. A December 2005 Gallup poll of Americans found that 57 percent said that they knew nothing or did not care about Muslim societies.

The High-level Group recommended that governments, multilateral institutions, universities and policy makers expand global, cross-cultural and human rights education through the following steps.

- Governments should ensure that their primary and secondary educational systems provide for a balance and integration of national history and identity formation with knowledge of other cultures, religions, and regions.

- Specialized agencies, such as UNESCO, should collaborate with educational research centres and curriculum developers on a regional basis to make existing resources in this field (such as the History of Humanity series and the Regional Histories Project) "classroom-ready" and to develop and implement a strategy for their dissemination and use by member states.

- Similarly, a strategy for the dissemination of human rights education materials should be developed, drawing on the work already achieved by UNESCO and on successful initiatives such as the Human Security Network's *Manual on Human Rights Education*.

- Public and private donors should provide research grants and funds for conferences and cross-regional exchanges to teacher training institutions at which specialists in world history and geography are developing content, pedagogy and teaching resources for world history curriculum.

- Public and private donors should support scholarly institutions to publish information about those parts of the Islamic heritage that deal with pluralism, rationality and the scientific method, and to make them available online in multiple languages.

- Public and private donors should support education efforts aimed at the general public in the West and in predominantly Muslim countries by funding arts performances, film festivals, educational tours, and scholarly and educational conferences that disseminate information on the richness of diverse cultures and on the importance of cultural interactions.

- Develop a joint public-private sector fund to support scholars engaged in teaching and researching cross-cultural dialogue and understanding.

The High-level Group also called for media literacy programs to be implemented in secondary schools to help develop a discerning and critical approach to news coverage. Also, religious leaders, education policy makers and interfaith organizations should develop consensus guidelines for teaching about religions. Curriculum review panels should be composed of the major faith traditions to review curricula for fairness, accuracy and balance in discussing religious beliefs. Multilateral organizations such as the Organization of the Islamic Conference and the European Union should emphasize intercultural tolerance and respect. Since only 18 per 1,000 people in the Middle East and North Africa have access to a computer (the global average is 73.8 per 1,000), governments and technology firms should collaborate to expand Internet access, with particular attention to predominantly Muslim countries. All of these steps would help to promote a well-rounded holistic education, which is invaluable for the development of critical thinking to prepare students for the complexities, ambiguities and constant change that characterize life in a multicultural world.

Expand Youth Opportunities

The High-level Group also focused on expanding opportunities for youth through student exchange programs, sports activities and political involvement. There is an urgent need to increase youth exchanges between young people of different cultural backgrounds, particularly Muslim and American. The United States, the European Union and the Organization of the Islamic Conference should subsidize these exchanges to allow participation by all levels of society, not just the elite.

Since the Middle East and North Africa have low rates of youth participation in the labour force (40 percent compared to a global average of 54 percent), new strategies to boost youth employment are needed. A coalition of key stakeholders should develop a youth employment strategy by greatly expanding the existing Youth Employment Network, a joint initiative of the UN, the World Bank and the International Labour Organization. Models of "one-stop shopping" for youth employment, including job training, resumé-writing and interview skills development, career counselling and microcredit financing have proven successful in several countries.

Muslim and Western public and private donors should address cultural alienation by establishing a cultural fund and networking service to connect young Muslim artists, writers, musicians and filmmakers with their Western counterparts and leaders in the culture industry. Also, religious leaders and civil society activists should establish a network of websites that link youth to religious scholars who can speak in constructive ways to the contemporary challenges facing youth. Such sites could feature discussion groups led by religious scholars providing interpretations of religious history and scripture that challenge exclusivist approaches.

Involving young people in community councils and the governing bodies of civil society organizations can provide them with unique platforms to take on constructive roles in their communities. Regional youth platforms, bringing together youth from diverse cultural, religious and national backgrounds, are a solid step towards an alliance of civilizations.

Women in Black

www.womeninblack.net

Women in Black is a movement of women committed to non-violence and non-aggression, both as a goal and as a means. Its "activism" takes the form of silent witness.

Women in Black vigils began in Israel in 1988 with women protesting Israel's occupation of the Gaza Strip and West Bank. Since then, Women in Black has formed in Spain, Azerbaijan, Germany, Italy, England, Canada, Colombia and the former Yugoslavia, where women in Belgrade have participated in weekly vigils since 1991 to protest war and the Serbian regime's policies of nationalist aggression. Slobodan Milosevic devoted many speeches to attacking the group, referring to members as "witches," indicating the effect the movement had on constraining his ability to act with impunity.

Since September 11, 2001, Women in Black movements have arisen in several cities in the US. The group expanded its witness in response to the 2003 invasion of Iraq. The international Women in Black movement continues to be strong nearly two decades after its creation. Although each movement is free to work towards its own goals and events, the national groups maintain communication and have annual international gatherings.

Special Difficulties of Migrants

Turning to the dynamics of migration, the High-level Group noted that virtually every nation is either a country of origin or of destination for immigrants. In a world of porous borders, quick transportation and communications, and globalized economies, diverse populations are destined to interact through continued migration, presenting new challenges to host countries. The solution to settlement problems is not to build walls around nations, but to start dealing with the reasons for mass migration. For example, if the wealthier countries lived up to their commitments of increased investment in and aid to the poorer countries, improved economic conditions would keep many potential migrants at home.

The group called attention to the special difficulties faced by Muslim immigrants in the US and Europe. Not only is it difficult to access education, social services, housing and jobs, but Muslims are also increasingly fearful of encroachments on their fundamental civil liberties. Developing mentoring programs to help both children and parental immigrants better understand laws, customs and how to get involved in society would help maximize integration. Establishing coherent integration strategies requires regular dialogue among representatives of government and immigrant communities as well as civil society groups. Concerted efforts would help to achieve a balance between the demands of integration and the need to maintain one's cultural and religious identity.

Overcoming Media Stereotyping

The media has the potential to serve as a bridge between cultures and societies. In fact, the High-level Group says, the power of words and images in shaping our understanding of the world cannot be overestimated. But the media, particularly in the West, is failing its responsibility. "In the West, an appreciably more nationalistic and at times anti-Muslim tone has become evident in news and commentary, especially since the events of 11 September, 2001."

Media stereotypes fuel conflict; the group proposed a host of actions to promote positive media portrayals of Muslims and cross-cultural dialogue. There is an urgent need for balanced images of ordinary Muslims in Western mass media. These could include, for example, publishing stories of successful and prominent Muslim women in the West, and about prominent Jewish human rights and social justice advocates in the Muslim world, and reprinting classics of Muslim and Western literature that counter prevailing stereotypes. Thus, the group calls for steps to increase objective reporting and the presentation of a diversity of perspectives to prevent stereotypes and misrepresentations from blocking the flow of reliable information.

The group devoted specific attention to the Internet. The Internet and digital media production and distribution have opened new avenues for media consumers to become media producers and provide vastly increased people-to-people communication. A new push to expand communication is essential to mobilize international public opinion on the values of an alliance of civilizations.

The group wound up its report by calling on the UN secretary-general to appoint a High Representative for the Alliance of Civilizations to oversee the implementation of the recommendations and also help to defuse religious and cultural tensions among communities in times of crisis. It also recommended that a forum for the alliance of civilizations be established under UN auspices to promote initiatives aimed at encouraging dialogue and building bridges among communities.

Global Conscience on a Large Canvas

The Alliance of Civilizations High-level Group reaches out to a world in which people respect one another's differences and jointly benefit from the progress of humanity. This is global conscience written on a very large canvas. Can we get there? Or will suspicions, hatred and greed pull us down just as we have the pinnacle in sight?

WITNESS

www.witness.org

WITNESS is an international human rights organization started by the tech-savvy musician Peter Gabriel that uses video technology to expose human rights abuses. WITNESS was born in 1992, not long after a video of Rodney King being assaulted by four Los Angeles police officers catalyzed interest in the use of video for human rights change. Today, WITNESS is an independent non-profit organization with offices in Brooklyn and New York and human rights partners around the world. The organization provides training and support to local groups for their human rights advocacy campaigns. Beyond providing video cameras and editing equipment, WITNESS is committed to facilitating exposure for partners' issues on a global scale. They help broker relationships with international media outlets, government officials, policymakers, activists and the general public so that once a video is made, it can be used as a tool to advocate for change.

Over the past decade, WITNESS has partnered with groups in more than 60 countries, bringing often unseen images, untold stories and seldom heard voices to the attention of decision makers, mass media and the public, thereby catalyzing grassroots activism, political engagement, and long-term change. WITNESS videos have been used to promote grassroots education and mobilization, to corroborate allegations of human rights violations, as a resource for news broadcasts, to catalyze human rights advocacy via the World Wide Web, as evidence in court and quasi-judicial hearings, to complement official written reports of human rights abuses, and as a deterrent to further abuse.

Kofi Annan, on receiving the report, said that these aspirations could not be reached if the current climate of fear and suspicion continues to be refuelled by political events, especially those in which Muslim peoples—Iraqis, Afghans, Chechens and Palestinians—are seen to be victims of military action by non-Muslim powers. The Arab-Israeli conflict, which has festered for so long, must somehow be settled, for no other conflict carries such a powerful symbolic and emotional charge among people far removed from the battlefield.

> As long as the Palestinians live under occupation, ex-posed to daily frustration and humiliation; and, as long as Israelis are blown up in buses and in dance halls: so long will passions everywhere be inflamed.

Annan said that it is imperative to work on both fronts at once, seeking to improve social and cultural understanding between peoples and, at the same time, resolving political conflicts in the Middle East and elsewhere. Of course, the killings of the moment must stop, but building conditions for long-term peace requires a new vision of the community of nations, freed from the scourge of ignorance and denial in which all forms of extremism find their source. The message that President Abdoulaye Wade of Senegal brought to the High-level Group is apt:

> Let us strive to ensure that each society, in a genuine effort toward reconciliation with others, can find the means to free itself from the prejudices and other per-sonal biases that lead it, often wrongly, to believe that it alone incarnates the best of civilization.

Thanks to the alliance of civilizations, we now understand better that there is no basis to the claim that civilizations are set on an inevitable collision course. Civilizations are not solid monoliths; rather, they result from complex mutual exchanges and constant cross-fertilization among cultural groups. Also, the history of relations between Muslim and Western societies is not primarily one of conflict. Despite periods of war, Islam, Christianity and Judaism all benefited from each other through trade and intellectual exchanges. The roots of the widening rift between Muslim and Western societies are not in religion or culture; rather, they are to be found in politics. This analysis led three members of the High-level Group—Archbishop Desmond Tutu, Ali Alatas of Indonesia and Andre Azoulay of Morocco—to warn leaders and shapers of public opinion to do everything in their power to promote mutual respect of religious beliefs and traditions, and especially to curb inflammatory language.

> We will achieve progress not by attempting to ignore or deny our differences, but by acknowledging them openly and by celebrating our diversity. We must also recognize that these differences are not primarily religious or cultural, but political. In other words, they are not insurmountable and can be overcome through determined leadership and sustained negotiations.

★ ★ ★

The power of the alliance of civilizations concept lies in its potential to transform the world from exclusive societies living independently of one another to inclusive societies comprising diverse people. "Different" people are no longer confined to distant lands. "Different" people are all around us. While the exigencies of our time forced the High-level Group to examine societal relationships through the prism of the divide between the West and Muslims, the true value of the report is that it speaks to the interrelationships of all humanity: "An Alliance of Civilizations must by nature be based on a multi-polar perspective."

The Universal Declaration of Human Rights and related documents, as well as the principles of international law, guided the work of the High-level Group. It took these well-established guidelines for humanity and applied them to the dangerous conditions of our time. It charted a path showing how human beings in the electronic age, in which we are all thrust together either physically or virtually, can reach our goals of self-determination in a non-violent manner.

That is why I said at the outset of this chapter that the transformative ideas of the culture of peace and the alliance of civilizations contain the seeds for a blossoming of humanity never seen before. When it is fully understood that all societies are bound together in their humanity and interdependent in their quest for stability, prosperity and peaceful co-existence, the maturation of all civilizations will take place.

Conclusion

Of Conscience, Critical Mass and Hope

Judging by the headlines of the summer and fall of 2006, when I was writing this book, my central point—that a global conscience is beginning to uplift humanity—would appear to be a risky proposition. The carnage in the Iraq war degenerated into butchery. The war in Afghanistan saw continued bombing and killing of innocent people. The rocket attacks between Hezbollah and Israel further inflamed the Middle East. Children continued to die from the effects of war, hunger and water-borne diseases. Global warming predictions worsened. Where is the global conscience?

To begin with, we cannot judge the state of the world only by the daily news. The media concentrate on confrontation. That is what they sell. And there is plenty of confrontation in the world. But what is lost in the headlines is the creativity of countless people to advance the human security agenda. Evil and misery are not inevitable. Voices are being raised against war, poverty, environmental damage and human rights violations. The voices have not yet reached a crescendo, but they are starting to shape public opinion.

The brutal killings in Iraq are probably not worse than what occurred in World War II, but a growing number of people, revolted by war, are resisting them. This has never happened before. Children and women have suffered the ravages of destitution for centuries, but the afflictions of the most vulnerable are now met with growing public compassion. Until half a century ago, human rights were barely recognized; now they are the subject of legislation in every country. Thirty years ago, the public hardly noticed the environment; in the crowded theatre where I saw Al Gore's *An Inconvenient Truth*, the audience applauded the film at the end.

Even Noam Chomsky, as trenchant a critic of US foreign policy as there is, says in his latest book, *Failed States*, "There has been substantial progress in the unending quest for justice and freedom in recent years, leaving a legacy that can be carried forward from a higher plane than before." Dr. Ron McCoy of Malaysia, former president of the International Physicians for the Prevention of Nuclear War, told the World Peace Forum in Vancouver in 2006, "Despite pessimists and 'realists,' there are signs of a worldwide change in awareness about politics and governance, about economies and ecology, about world peace, disarmament and conflict resolution, and about the partnership and interdependence between men and women." Former US President Bill Clinton draws together 1000 leaders of business, government and civil society in annual meetings of the Clinton Global Initiative to develop and fund practical plans to deal with climate change, global health, poverty, and religious and ethnic conflict. (Clinton insists that attendees fulfill commitments and are not invited back when they do not.)

Opinion about the human condition is turning. This may be due to fear—of a global catastrophe caused by terrorists, a nuclear war or the rising of the oceans from global warming. But it may also be that an awakened view of the need for a more harmonious planet is, indeed, taking hold. Both negative and positive influences shape conscience. What is clear is that an awakened global conscience is questioning, probing and challenging existing world systems.

These systems have always been dominated by the rich and militarily powerful and, for the past 350 years, national interests have always prevailed. Now, globalization is breaking down national interests, and the lightning speed of mass global communication is empowering people all over the world. There is not yet a map to human security, at least that everyone can agree on. So there is much disorder, confusion and ranting. But there are also global strategies for disarmament, sustainable development, the protection of the environment and the advancement of human rights, produced by the UN.

These strategies are not yet being advocated sufficiently powerfully to overcome an unjust world economy, world disorder and the undermining of human rights and the rule of law. Perhaps the world will still have to endure genocidal civil wars in the Middle East, more religious extremism and a wave of nuclear proliferation. But the very forces of nature, business, communication and world politics are building up a single society. The chief characteristic of the society is its common humanity. Civilizations are struggling to live at peace in the single society.

The global conscience that is now identified in every civilization will help to move humanity forward. By moving forward, I mean reaching the day when it becomes cultural, not countercultural, to stand in the public square and demand an end to war, an end to nuclear weapons and an end to massive poverty, and demand that the full weight of government policies and finances be directed to building the conditions for peace. These thoughts are not just wishful thinking; they are firmly implanted in the minds of the millions of people who belong to the organizations I have sketched in the vignettes throughout this book.

Cynicism always seems to be in fashion. But cynics today cannot match the power of a critical mass of people across the planet awakened to a new understanding that civil society networking can prod governments to move forward on equitable policies for food distribution, clean water availability, decent sanitation, properly equipped medical clinics and sufficiently funded education systems. Critical thinking can move the leaders of commerce to accept that sustainable business is good business, and that protecting the environment is not a cost issue but a human survival issue.

Many are showing a new appreciation of the need for a strengthened international legal order, a reformed United Nations and genuine participatory democracy. Many are clamouring for a world in which women are fully empowered and equally represented in decision-making processes. Many are working for an alliance of civilizations, in which the spiritual aspirations of believers are celebrated.

Global conscience keeps driving us forward to a world of greater care and mutual respect. Violence, war and greed still assault us. But the body of humanity, elevated in its spirit, mind and capacity to act, grows stronger. The stirring and movement of this body provide new hope for humanity.

Chapter Notes

Chapter 1

A basic reference work for the subject of global conscience is *Globalization and Catholic Social Thought: Present Crisis, Future Hope*, John A. Coleman and William F. Ryan, eds. (Novalis, 2005). It provides the basic material for, in the words of the editors, "a bold, credible and consistent ecclesial call for justice in an emerging world order (or disorder, as it may become)." The *Encyclopedia of Religion*, Second Edition, contains an excellent summary of how conscience has been viewed through the ages. St. Paul's Letter to the Romans, in particular 13:1-7, is very instructive. Some modern works I found helpful include *The Call of Conscience*, Michael J. Hyde (University of South Carolina Press, 2001); *Conscience and Other Virtues*, Douglas C. Langston (The Pennsylvania State University Press, 2001); and *Conscience and Its Critics*, Edward G. Andrew (University of Toronto Press, 2001).

Chapter 2

The debate in the UN General Assembly on a dialogue among civilizations took place on November 8 and 9, 2001. It is available at www.un.org/spanish/aboutun/organs/ga/56/verbatim/a56pv40.pdf. See also www.un.org/Dialogue for an excellent description of the UN dialogue process. The article "How to Prevent a Clash of Civilizations" by Hans Küng, published in the *International Herald Tribune*, March 4–5, 2006, is excellent. "The Party at Davos," by Jeff Faux, published in *The Nation,* February 13, 2006, is a strong critique of economic globalization. The Research Branch of the Parliamentary Library in Ottawa provided me with many articles on the subject. The following books were helpful: *Global Visions: Beyond the New World Order*, Jeremy Brecker, John Brown Childs and Jill Carter, eds. (South End Press, Boston, 1993); *Globalization and Its Victims*, Jon Sobrino and Felix Wilfred, eds. (Concilium, SCM Press, London, 2001); and *In Search of Universal Values*, Karl-Josef Kuschel and Dietmar Mieth, eds. (Concilium, SCM Press, London, 2001).

Chapter 3

Four interrelated UN documents provide the background for the ideas in this chapter on the new understanding of security: *A More Secure World: Our Shared Responsibility*, the Report of the Secretary-General's High-level Panel on Threats, Challenges and Change (United Nations, 2004); *In Larger Freedom: Towards Development, Security and Human Rights for All*, Report of the Secretary-General, March 21, 2005 (UN Document A/59/2005); *2005 World Summit Outcome*, October 25, 2005 (UN Document A/RES/60/1); and *Implementation of Decisions from the 2005 World Summit Outcome for Action by the Secretary-General*, October 25, 2005 (UN Document A/60/430). A critique of the 60th anniversary summit document is found in *United Nations World Summit: Major Achievements, Failures and Postponements*, published by the World Federalist Movement, Canada, October 2005. The work of the many UN commissions of the past three decades is fully reported in two of my previous books: *Building Global Security: An Agenda for the 1990s* (NC Press Ltd., Toronto, 1999) and *A Bargain for Humanity* (University of Alberta Press, 1993). I also found *International Commissions and the Power of Ideas* (Ramesh Thakur, Andrew F. Cooper and John English, eds.), published by United Nations University Press (Tokyo, New York, Paris, 2005), helpful in evaluating the UN commissions. An excellent resource on the issues surrounding the idea of a permanent UN peace-making force is *A United Nations Emergency Peace Service*, Robert C. Johansen, ed., published by Global Action to Prevent War, Nuclear Age Peace Foundation and World Federalist Movement, 2006. In his preface, Sir Brian Urquhart pays tribute to Peter Langille of the University of Western Ontario for his pioneering work on the subject. *The Responsibility to Protect*, the Report of the International Commission on Intervention and State Sovereignty, sponsored by the Government of Canada, provides important background information on the subject. General Romeo Dallaire's graphic account of the genocide in Rwanda is contained in his book, *Shake Hands with the Devil: The Failure of Humanity in Rwanda,* Vintage Canada, 2003.

Chapter 4

In his introduction to the *Human Security Report 2005*, Archbishop Desmond Tutu writes, "In a world where war, terrorism and humanitarian crises can seem all-pervasive, the *Human Security Report* offers a rare message of hope." That is the way I feel about the report, which tracks the extraordinary changes taking place in global security. I have quoted from the report and a brief follow-up document issued in 2006 with permission from the Human Security Centre of the University of British Columbia. The 2005 report is published by Oxford University Press, New York. It is very instructive to read the *Human Security Report* alongside *Weapons of Terror: Freeing the World of Nuclear, Biological and Chemical Arms,* the 2006 report of the Weapons of Mass Destruction Commission, headed by the Swedish diplomat Hans Blix. As Blix hints, the 60 recommendations in his report can only be fully implemented "when there is a greater readiness to return to a cooperative multilateral system in the sphere of arms control and disarmament." The UN Small Arms Conference, July 2006, has been fully reported by the International Action Network for Small Arms (www.iansa.org) and analyzed by Mary Robinson, former UN High Commissioner for Human Rights, in *The Guardian*, July 11, 2006. The UN Secretary-General gave his "sleepwalking" speech on May 18, 2006, at the University of Tokyo, Japan (www.u-tokyo.ac.jp/public/archive_e.html, accessed April 3, 2007). The report of the Carnegie Commission on Preventing Deadly Conflict is found at http://wwics.si.edu/subsites/ccpdc/pubs/rept97/finfr.htm. Global Action to Prevent War has an excellent program statement (www.globalactionpw.org), which, in 2006 was updated by

Jonathan Dean, who kindly sent me updated material. The report of the 2006 UN conference held by the Global Partnership for the Prevention of Armed Conflict is available c/o European Centre for Conflict Prevention, PO Box 14069, 3508SC Utrecht, The Netherlands or info@conflict-prevention.net. The companion book, *People Building Peace II: Successful Stories of Civil Society*, is the source of the two stories of successful peace-building in Croatia and Liberia. The publisher, Lynne Rienner in Boulder, Colorado, gave permission to use this material. The developing role of women in the prevention and resolution of conflict is fully examined in *Beyond Conflict Prevention: How Women Prevent Violence and Build Sustainable Peace*, by Camille Pampell Conaway and Anjalina Sen, published by Global Action to Prevent War and Women's International League for Peace and Freedom, 2005.

Chapter 5

The video *Why We Fight,* analyzing the power of the military-industrial complex, won the grand jury prize for documentaries at the 2005 Sundance Film Festival in Utah. It was made by Eugene Jerecki for the BBC and runs 100 minutes. World military expenditures are tracked annually by the Stockholm International Peace Research Institute; I have used figures from this organization's 2006 yearbook. More information about US spending is provided by William Rivers Pitt in "Banking on War" (Truthout: www.truthout.org/docs_2006/080206Z.shtml). A comprehensive examination of US spending on nuclear arms is contained in *Atomic Audit*, Stephen I. Schwartz, ed. (Brookings Institution Press, Washington, D.C., 1998). The figures illustrating the impact of military spending on Chicago are found in material published by the National Priorities Project, 17 New South Street, Suite 302, Northampton, MA 01060. *The End of Poverty* by Jeffrey D. Sachs (The Penguin Press, New York, 2005) is, as mentioned in the chapter, an otherwise excellent book on ending poverty but for the serious omission of the effect of military spending. The UN General Assembly has passed many resolutions on the relationship between disarmament and development; the latest (A/RES/60/61) was adopted December 8, 2005. I have drawn from the report of the Group of Governmental Experts, *The Relationship Between Disarmament and Development in the Current International Context,* June 23, 2004 (A/59/119). It deserves far more public attention than it has received so far. The Year 2000 Campaign to Redirect World Military Spending to Human Development deserves the attention of the thoughtful public, although it, too, has been marginalized by the stream of global crises. The campaign was launched in December 1995. I have used material from Oscar Arias's speech to the Development Policy Forum of the German Foundation for International Development, October 31, 2000. Jayantha Dhanapala's description of "sustainable disarmament for sustainable development" is in a speech he gave to the Lalith Athulathmudali Foundation in Colombo, Sri Lanka, in 1998.

Chapter 6

The two Gore books on the environmental crisis demonstrate the former vice-president's passionate commitment to preserving planetary life: *Earth in the Balance* (Houghton Mifflin Company, New York, 1992) and *An Inconvenient Truth* (Rodale, Emmaus, PA, 2006). It is interesting to note that, in his first book, Gore wrote, "... it became clear to me that we have to consider the complex nature of our interaction with the *whole* environment; more specifically, I zeroed in on the central importance of our way of thinking about that relationship." Sir David King's comments were published in *Science,* January 9, 2004. James Hansen described the effects of climate change in "The Threat to the Planet," published in *The New York Review of Books,* July 13, 2006. Both King's and Hansen's views are elaborated on in "A Graver Threat Than Terrorism: Global Warming," *Vanity Fair,* May 2006. An excellent source for technical detail is found in "Global Warming: Bulletins from a Warmer World," *National Geographic,* September 2004. The report of the International Panel on Climate Change is found at www.ipcc.ch. A full description of the dangers of nuclear power is contained in *Insurmountable Risks: Can Nuclear Power Solve the Global Warming Problem?* by Brice Smith, published by the Institute for Energy and Environmental Research, Takoma Park, Maryland, August 2006. The Massachusetts

Institute of Technology study is contained in *The Future of Nuclear Power*, 2003 (http://web.mit.edu/nuclearpower/pdf/nuclearpower-full.pdf). Jeffrey Sach's comments on the effect of global warming are in *Scientific American*, June 2006. One of the best descriptions of how the environmental crisis fits into the entire picture of sustainable security is contained in *Global Responses to Global Threats: Sustainable Security for the 21st Century*, by Chris Abbott, Paul Rogers and John Sloboda, published by the Oxford Research Group, 2006. Material on the Earth Charter can be found at www.earthcharter.org.

Chapter 7

My earlier book *United Nations, Divided World* was published by NC Press in 1984. The list of examples of the UN's accomplishments is drawn from *60 Ways the United Nations Makes a Difference*, published by the United Nations Department of Public Information, 2005 (Sales No. 05.1.91). The policy analysis brief *United Nations Reform in Context*, published by the Stanley Foundation, Muscatine, Iowa, provides an excellent overview of the ongoing efforts to reform the UN. Again, in this chapter, the valuable material in the Report of the Secretary-General's High-level Panel on Threats, Challenges and Change, the Annan responses and the 2005 World Summit Outcome document, all referred to earlier in the book, have guided my presentation of the current situation of the UN. I advise students who may be studying the complexities of the UN to read the three documents together. The literature on the UN is vast, not to mention the numerous links offered at www.un.org. Two recent books that I have found helpful are *The Parliament of Man: The Past, Present, and Future of the United Nations* by Paul Kennedy (Harper Collins, Toronto, 2006) and *Social Justice in an Open World: The Role of the United Nations*, published by the UN Department of Economic and Social Affairs, 2006.

Chapter 8

A stimulating overview of the world's major religions and what they all contribute to peace is found in *World Religions—Universal Peace—Global Ethic* by Hans Küng, one of the outstanding theologians of modern times, published by the Global Ethic Foundation, Tübingen, Germany. An exhibit on this theme has been shown around the world. Küng is a prominent advocate of inter-religious dialogue and a chief figure in the World's Parliament of Religions. His earlier book *Global Responsibility: In Search of a New World Ethic* (Crossroad, New York, 1991) has influenced my thinking through the years. The Kyoto Declaration on Confronting Violence and Advancing Shared Security was issued by the Religions for Peace Eighth World Assembly, August, 2006 (www.wcrp.org). The informative article "God's Country" by Walter Russell Mead discusses how the evangelical boom is remaking US politics; it was published in *Foreign Affairs,* September/October 2006. More information about how the "moral values" debate divides the American electorate is contained in *Faith and Politics,* by Senator John Danforth (Viking, 2006). A similar analysis of the Christian Right is contained in *Our Endangered Values* by former US President Jimmy Carter (Simon and Schuster, 2005). The Permanent Mission of the Republic of the Philippines to the United Nations provided me with background information on the Inter-Faith Dialogue, which a number of states are conducting at the United Nations. (See UN Document A/61/492, October 3, 2006). The dialogue deserves to be better known by the public. More information can be found at www.tripartiteinterfaithforum.org.

The quotations from Vatican II documents are from *The Documents of Vatican II,* Walter M. Abbott, SJ, ed. (Angelus, 1966). The *Compendium of the Social Doctrine of the Church* was produced by the Pontifical Council for Justice and Peace (Libreria Editorice Vaticana, 2004) and is available from Canadian Conference of Catholic Bishops Publications Service (1-800-769-1147 or www.cccbpublications.ca). An analysis of "Ethical Reflections" 20 years after it was issued was published by William J. Ryan, SJ, in *Catholic New Times*, February 9, 2003.

Chapter 9

In 2005, UN Secretary-General Kofi Annan, deeply concerned about cultural polarization in the world, established a group of eminent personalities and tasked it with generating a report containing an analysis of the rise in cross-cultural polarization and extremism and a set of practical recommendations to counter this phenomenon. The High-level Group on the Alliance of Civilizations met five times from November 2005 to November 2006, and produced a report that takes a multi-polar approach within which it prioritizes relations between Muslim and Western societies. It is available at www.unaoc.org. The members of the High-level Group were as follows:

Turkey

Prof. Mehmet Aydin, Co-chair, Minister of State of Turkey and Professor of Philosophy

Spain

Prof. Federico Mayor, Co-chair, President, Culture of Peace Foundation, and Former Director-General, UNESCO

Middle East

Seyyed Mohammad Khatami (Iran), Former President of Iran

Her Highness Sheikha Mozah bint Nasser al Missned (Qatar), Consort of the Emir, State of Qatar, and Chairperson, Qatar Foundation for Education, Science and Community Development

Dr. Ismail Serageldin (Egypt), President, Bibliotheca Alexandrina

North Africa

Dr. Mohamed Charfi (Tunisia), Former Education Minister of Tunisia

André Azoulay (Morocco), Adviser to King Mohammed VI of Morocco

West Africa

Moustapha Niasse, Former Prime Minister of Senegal

Southern Africa

Archbishop Desmond Tutu, Archbishop of Cape Town

West Europe

Hubert Védrine (France), Former Minister of Foreign Affairs

Karen Armstrong (UK), Historian of Religion

East Europe

Prof. Vitaly Naumkin (Russia), President of the International Center for Strategic and Political Studies, and Chair, Moscow State University

North America

Prof. John Esposito (US), Founding Director, Prince Al-Waleed bin-Talal Center for Muslim-Christian Understanding (Georgetown University), Editor-in-Chief, *Oxford Encyclopedia of the Islamic World*

Rabbi Arthur Schneier (US), President, Appeal of Conscience Foundation, and Senior Rabbi, East Park Synagogue

Latin America

Enrique Iglesias (Uruguay), Secretary-General, Ibero-American Organization, and Former President, Inter-American Development Bank

Prof. Candido Mendes (Brazil), Secretary-General, Académie de la Latinité

South Asia

Dr. Nafis Sadik (Pakistan), Special Adviser to the UN Secretary-General

Shobhana Bhartia (India), Member of Parliament, India Vice Chairperson and Editorial Director, *Hindustan Times*, New Delhi

South East Asia

Ali Alatas, Former Foreign Minister of Indonesia

East Asia

Prof. Pan Guang (China), Director and Professor, Shanghai Academy of Social Sciences.

Index of Proper Names and Organizations

A

Abolition 2000 76, 148
Afghanistan 53, 62, 67, 78, 90, 133, 134, 176, 182, 183, 192, 195
Africa 26, 33, 53, 70, 73, 83, 85, 94, 111, 142, 146, 180, 186, 187
Agenda 21 113
Agenda for Peace, An 56
Al Qaeda 182
Alatas, Ali 192
Albright, Madeleine 139
Aleksa, Dragica 83, 84
Algeria 31, 36
Amnesty International 42
Angola 134
Annan, Kofi 36, 53–54, 58–60, 63–64, 68, 73, 77, 81, 131, 139, 143, 145, 147, 177–178, 192
Antarctica 111
Anti-Personnel Landmines Treaty 61
Arab world 177
Argentina 73
Arias, Oscar 102–103
Arias Foundation for Peace and Human Progress 102
Armenia 37
Armstrong, Karen 179
Article VI Forum 76
Asia 53, 111, 146, 162, 180
Atomic Audit 90
Axworthy, Lloyd 68
Aydin, Mehmet 178–179
Azoulay, André 193

B

Balkans 181
Bangladesh 111
Benedict XVI, Pope 158–159
Berak 83
Berlin Wall 18, 52
Bible 35, 158, 160
Blix, Hans 67–68, 72
Bolton, John 60
Bosnia 78, 134, 135
Boutros-Ghali, Boutros 56, 130, 131, 139
Brandt, Willy 49
Brazil 107, 143
Brookings Institute 90
Brundtland, Gro Harlem 51, 54
Buddhism 27
Building Resources Across Communities 127
Burkina Faso 36
Burma 31
Burma Watch International 184
Burundi 81, 86
Bush administration 60, 91, 116, 139
Bush, George W. 156

C

Calvin, John 25
Cambodia 62, 132, 135, 181
Canada 38, 57, 107
Canadian Conference of Catholic Bishops 173
Carlsson, Ingvar 52
Carnegie Commission on Preventing Deadly Conflict 78, 79

Carson, Rachel 113
Carter, Jimmy 155
Catholicism 159, 165–174
Central Emergency Revolving
    Fund 98
Centre for Peace, Non-Violence
    and Human Rights 83, 85
Chechnya 31, 192
Chernobyl 117
China 36, 73, 107, 116, 119, 142
Chomsky, Noam 196
Christian Right 155–157
Christianity *see also* Christians
    154–155, 157, 171–172, 181,
    193
Christians *see also* Christianity
    23–27, 159–160
Civil Society Panel 145, 146
Clash of Civilizations, The 176–
    177
Clinton, Bill 196
Clinton Global Initiative 196
Cold War 17, 51, 67, 71, 76, 89,
    91, 93, 97, 101, 165–166
Coleman, John A. 41–42
Commission of Sustainable
    Development 128
*Compendium of the Social Doctrine
    of the Church* 172
Conference on the Environment
    113
Conference on Inter-faith
    Cooperation for Peace 160
Conference on the Relationship
    Between Disarmament and
    Development 51, 95
Congo 81, 82
Costa Rica 73
Croatia 83, 85
*Crossing the Divide: Dialogue
    Among Civilizations* 176
Crusades 27, 177
Cuba 73

Culture of Peace Foundation
    178

D

Dallaire, Roméo 63, 137
Darfur 12, 62, 82, 125, 182
de Roo, Bishop Remi 173
Declaration and Programme of
    Action on a Culture of Peace
    176
Dhanapala, Jayantha 102, 103–
    104

E

Earth Charter 128–130
Earth in the Balance 109
Earth Summit 113, 130
East Timor 72, 132
Ecuador 125
Einstein, Albert 77
Eisenhower, Dwight 88–89, 90,
    91
El Nino 125
El Salvador 132, 133
End of Poverty, The 95
Enlightenment 181
Erdogan, Recep Tayyip 177
Eritrea 132
*Ethical Reflections on the Economic
    Crisis* 173
Europe 189
European Centre for Conflict
    Prevention 81
European Union 31, 81, 187
Evans, Gareth 64

F

Failed States 196
Faithful Security 164
Falk, Richard 41
Finland 73
France 73, 107, 142

G

G8 40, 107
Gambia 84
Gaudium et Spes 167–168
Germany 107, 143
Global Action to Prevent War 70,
   80–81
Global Partnership for the
   Prevention of Armed Conflict
   81, 82–83
Global Security Institute 50
Global Youth Action 79
*Globalization and Catholic Social
   Thought* 42
Google Earth 44
Gorbachev, Mikhail 17–18, 128
Gore, Al 109–110, 123–124, 196
Gospels 23
Grameen Bank 92
Greenland 111
Guatemela 133
Guinea-Bissau 84
Gulf War 52

H

Hannay, David 54
Hansen, James 111
Hartung, William D. 89
Havel, Vaclav 18
Hello Peace 86
Helms, Jesse 139
Hezbollah 53, 67, 70, 195
High Commission for Refugees
   134
High-level Group on the
   Alliance of Civilizations 40.
   175, 178–181, 183, 184–194
High-level Panel on Threats,
   Challenges and Change 54,
   59–60, 62, 64, 67, 72, 119, 121,
   140, 142, 143, 145
Hinduism 27
Hiroshima 76, 117
History of Humanity series 185

HIV/AIDS 54, 59, 98, 124, 132,
   134
Holocaust 181
Holy See 39
Human Development Report 101
Human Rights Commission 144
Human Rights Watch 32
Human Security Centre 68
Human Security Network 185
Human Security Report 68
Humanae Vitae 171
Huntington, Samuel 176–177
Hussein, Saddam 138
Hutus 62

I

In Larger Freedom 58–59
Inconvenient Truth, An 109–110,
   196
Independent Inquiry on Rwanda
   63
India 73, 107, 116, 142, 143
Institute for Multi-Track
   Diplomacy 75
Inter-Faith Action for People in
   Africa 161
Inter-Faith Forum 162
Intergovernmental Authority on
   Development 82
Intergovernmental Panel on
   Climate Change 111
International Atomic Energy
   Agency 133
International Campaign to Ban
   Landmines 85
International Court of Justice 72
International Criminal Court 19,
   38, 61, 179
International Decade for a
   Culture of Peace and Non-
   violence for the Children of
   the World 53, 176
International Labour
   Organization 187

International Monetary Fund 40, 107

International Network for Conflict Resolution Education and Peace Education 82–83

International Panel on Climate Change 115

International Peace Bureau 95

International Physicians for the Prevention of Nuclear War 196

International Society for Research on Aggression 79

Inter-Parliamentary Union 147

Iran 73, 119, 133

Iraq 19, 31, 53, 61, 62, 66, 70, 78, 89, 133, 138, 139, 156, 176, 182, 183, 192, 195

Islam *see also* Muslims 27, 36–37, 154–155, 157, 159, 181, 193

Islamophobia 182

Israel 53, 67, 70, 73, 86, 124, 182, 183, 195

Italy 107

J

JAMMA 86

Japan 73, 107, 143

Jews *see also* Judaism 156–157, 158, 190

John XXIII, Pope 167

John Paul II, Pope 165–167, 169–170, 171

Judaism *see also* Jews 27, 181, 193

K

Kaplan, Fred 90–91

Kasper, Cardinal Walter 158

Kennedy, John F. 17, 18

Kennedy, Paul 151

Kenya 73, 81

Khatanu, Mohamed 179

Khatemi, Mohammed 35–36

Khmer Rouge 62

Khrushchev, Nikita 17

Ki-Moon, Ban 145

King, Sir David 111

Koran 35, 158, 160

Kosovo 52, 132

Kruhonja, Katarina 83

Kuwait 52

Kyoto Protocol 19, 61, 114–116, 119–121, 122

L

Lappe, Frances Moore 33

Latin America 73, 146, 180

League of Nations 147

Lebanon 62

Liberia 84, 161

Limited Test Ban Treaty 17

London 53

Luther, Martin 25

M

Mack, Andrew 68–71

Madrid 53, 177

Malawi 124

Mali 84

Manual on Human Rights Education 185

Martin, Lawrence 29

Martin, Paul 29

Martino, Cardinal Renato 172

Massachusetts Institute of Technology 121–122

Mayor, Federico 176, 178–179

McCoy, Ron 196

Mexico 37, 107, 143

Middle East 61, 117, 156, 162, 176, 180, 186, 187, 192, 195, 197

Middle Powers Initiative 53, 76

Millennium Declaration 19

Millennium Development Goals 19, 59, 95, 96, 107, 120, 132, 137, 149, 163

Montreal Protocol 133

Mozambique 132, 134

Muslims *see also* Islam 156–157, 177, 181–186, 187, 189–190, 193

N

Nagasaki 76
Nairobi 82
Namibia 132
National Priorities Project 92–93
NATO 89
Nepal 31
Netherlands 98
Nicaragua 132
Niger 124
Nigeria 84, 143
Non-Proliferation Treaty *see* Nuclear Non-Proliferation Treaty
North Korea 119
North-South: A Programme for Survival 49
Northern Ireland 86
Nostra Aetate 159
Nuclear Non-Proliferation Treaty 19, 61, 76, 80, 119, 140–141

O

Office of Net Assessment 111
Organization of the Islamic Conference 187
Our Endangered Values 155
Oxford Research Group 126–127

P

P5 140, 142–143
Pacem in Terris 167
Pakistan 73
Palestine 86, 182, 183, 192
Palme, Olof 49–50, 51
Palme Commission 51–52
Panyarachun, Anand 54

Parents Circle-Families Forum 86
Parliament of the World's Religions 163
Parliamentarians for Global Action 112
Parliamentary Network for Nuclear Disarmament 118
Partners in Development 49
Paul VI, Pope 169, 171
Pax Christi 170
Peace and Reconciliation Group 86
Pearson, Lester B. 49
Pearson Commission 49
PeaceJam 123
Peace Boat 58
People Building Peace II: Successful Stories of Civil Society 83
Perez de Cuellar, Javier 131
Permanent Forum on Indigenous Issues 135
Philippines 160, 161
Pontifical Council for Justice and Peace 169, 172
Pope, the 25
Populorum Progressio 169, 171
Pot, Pol 62
Primakov, Yevgeny 54
Pro Mujer 94
Project Ploughshares 67, 97
Pugwash 77

Q

Quakers *see* Religious Society of Friends

R

Ramphal, Shridath 52
Reformation, Protestant 25
Regional Histories Project 185
Religious Society of Friends 163
Renaissance 181

Rio Earth Summit 128
Romulo, Alberto G. 161
Rural Southern Voice for Peace 83
Russell, Bertrand 77
Russia 73, 107, 142
Rwanda 55, 62, 78, 81, 133, 135, 137, 181

S

Sachs, Jeffrey 95, 124
St. Paul 23, 25
Saudi Arabia 36
Scandinavia 98
Schwartz, Stephen I. 90
Scientific Conference on the Conservation and Utilization of Resources 112–113
Scowcroft, Brent 54
Scriptures, Hebrew 25
Search for Common Ground 47
Second Vatican Council 26, 159, 165, 167–168, 171, 173
Senegal 84
September 11, 2001 18–19, 27, 35, 52, 53, 55, 91, 103, 155, 156, 158, 176, 177, 182, 189
Serbia 52, 62
Seville Statement on Violence 78
Shias 182
Sierra Leone 72, 161
Silent Spring 113
Slavonia 83
Small Planet Institute 33
Somalia 52, 78
South Africa 107, 132, 143
South America 142
Soviet Union 17, 18, 166, 181
Star Wars 89
Strong, Maurice 114, 128
Sudan 81, 82, 134
Sunnis 182

T

Taliban 182
Taylor, Charles 84
Thailand 124
Thorsson, Inga 50–51, 96
Thorsson group 51
Torah 158, 160
Transparency International 178
Tubman, Harriet 84
Turkey 177
Tutsis 62
Tutu, Archbishop Desmond 179, 193

U

Uganda 81, 82
UNESCO 80, 133, 176, 185
UNICEF 132
Union of Concerned Scientists 111
United Kingdom 73, 107, 142
United Nations *see also* individual UN agencies 12, 15, 20, 28, 34, 41, 46–49, 71–72, 95, 96, 131–151, 187, 197; Development Fund for Women 134; Development Programme 95, 107, 132; Environment Programme 113; Industrial Development Organization 134; Peacekeeping 136; Security Council 55–57, 62, 64, 71, 73, 78, 80, 86, 89, 135–136, 138–139, 140–143; 60th anniversary summit document 175
United States 12, 17, 19, 29, 38, 51, 53, 60–61, 63, 83, 88–90, 92–93, 95, 98, 107, 109, 111, 114, 115, 116, 120, 123, 139, 147, 156, 166, 176, 182, 187, 189, 196

Universal Declaration of Human
  Rights 28, 39, 132, 162, 171,
  193

V

Volker, Paul 138

W

Wade, Abdoulaye 160, 192
Waldheim, Kurt 131
Weapons of Mass Destruction
  Commission 67–68
Western world 27, 36, 37–39,
  142, 155–157, 162, 176, 177,
  179, 181–183, 186, 189–190,
  193
Why We Fight 88
WITNESS 191
Women in Black 188
Women in Peacebuilding
  Network (WIPNET) 84, 85
World Bank 71, 107, 187
World Conference of Religions
  for Peace 159
World Council of Churches 163
World Day of Peace 169
World Federation of UN
  Associations 141
World Health Organization 111
World Hunger Year 105
World Peace Forum 196
World Religions for Peace
  Conference 163
World Social Forum 19
World Trade Center 156
World Trade Organization 49
World War II 147, 195

Y

Year 2000 Campaign to Redirect
  World Military Spending to
  Human Development 102–103
Year of Dialogue Among
  Civilizations 176
Youth Employment Network
  187
Yugoslav war 52, 83
Yugoslavia (former) 133

Z

Zapatero, Rodriguez 177

Hon. Douglas Roche, OC

The Hon. Douglas Roche, OC, is an author, parliamentarian and diplomat who, throughout his 35-year public career, has specialized in peace and human security issues.

Mr. Roche has been a senator, member of Parliament, Canadian Ambassador for Disarmament and Visiting Professor at the University of Alberta. He was elected Chairman of the United Nations Disarmament Committee at the 43rd General Assembly in 1988.

The author of 18 books, his latest is *Global Conscience* (Novalis, 2007). A previous book, *The Human Right to Peace* (Novalis, 2003), was the Canadian Book Review Annual Editor's Choice scholarly selection for July–August 2005. He has contributed chapters to 17 additional books.

Mr. Roche holds seven honorary doctorates from Canadian and American universities and has received numerous awards for his work for peace and non-violence, including the Mahatma Gandhi Foundation for World Peace Award (Canada) and the United Nations Association's Medal of Honour. In 1995, Pope John Paul II presented him with the Papal Medal for his service as special adviser on disarmament and security matters. In 1998, the Holy See named him a Knight Commander of the Order of St. Gregory the Great. He received the 2003 Peace Award of the Canadian Islamic Congress and the 2005 Luminosa Award for Unity from the Focolare Movement, North America. In 2005, he was given Lifetime Achievement awards from both the Canadian Pugwash Group and the Nuclear Age Peace Foundation. Pax Christi Ireland gave him its Peace Award in 2007. He is an Officer of the Order of Canada.

Mr. Roche is Chairman of the Middle Powers Initiative, an international network of seven non-governmental organizations specializing in nuclear disarmament issues. He is a member of the Pugwash Council, which won the 1995 Nobel Peace Prize for its work for nuclear disarmament.

E-mail: djroche@shaw.ca
Website: www.douglasroche.ca

Books by Douglas Roche

The Catholic Revolution (McKay, 1968)

Man to Man (Bruce, 1969), with Bishop Remi De Roo

It's a New World (Western Catholic Reporter, 1970)

Justice Not Charity: A New Global Ethic for Canada (McClelland and Stewart Ltd., 1976)

The Human Side of Politics (Clarke, Irwin, 1976)

What Development Is All About: China, Indonesia, Bangladesh (NC Press, 1979)

Politicians for Peace (NC Press, 1983)

United Nations: Divided World (NC Press, 1984)

Building Global Security: Agenda for the 1990s (NC Press, 1989)

In the Eye of the Catholic Storm (HarperCollins 1992), with Bishop Remi De Roo and Mary Jo Leddy

A Bargain for Humanity: Global Security by 2000 (University of Alberta Press, 1993)

Safe Passage into the Twenty-First Century: The United Nations' Quest for Peace, Equality, Justice and Development (Continuum, 1995), with Robert Muller

An Unacceptable Risk: Nuclear Weapons in a Volatile World (Project Ploughshares, 1995)

The Ultimate Evil: The Fight to Ban Nuclear Weapons (Lorimer, 1997)

Bread Not Bombs: A Political Agenda for Social Justice (University of Alberta Press, 1999)

The Human Right to Peace (Novalis, 2003)

Beyond Hiroshima (Novalis, 2005)